15

HANDBOOK OF THE
COLLECTION OF
MUSICAL INSTRUMENTS
IN THE UNITED STATES
NATIONAL MUSEUM

Da Capo Press Music Reprint Series

GENERAL EDITOR

FREDERICK FREEDMAN

VASSAR COLLEGE

HANDBOOK OF THE COLLECTION OF MUSICAL INSTRUMENTS IN THE UNITED STATES NATIONAL MUSEUM

By Frances Densmore

𝄢 DA CAPO PRESS • NEW YORK • 1971

A Da Capo Press Reprint Edition

This Da Capo Press edition of
*Handbook of the Collection of Musical Instruments
in the United States National Museum*
is an unabridged republication of the first
edition published in Washington, D. C., in 1927
as Bulletin 136 of the Smithsonian Institution.

Library of Congress Catalog Card Number 79-155231

SBN 306-70167-7

Published by Da Capo Press, Inc.
A Subsidiary of Plenum Publishing Corporation
227 West 17th Street, New York, N. Y. 10011

Manufactured in the United States of America

SMITHSONIAN INSTITUTION

UNITED STATES NATIONAL MUSEUM

Bulletin 136

HANDBOOK OF THE COLLECTION OF MUSICAL INSTRUMENTS IN THE UNITED STATES NATIONAL MUSEUM

BY

FRANCES DENSMORE

Collaborator, Bureau of American Ethnology, Smithsonian Institution

UNITED STATES
GOVERNMENT PRINTING OFFICE
WASHINGTON
1927

ADVERTISEMENT

The scientific publications of the National Museum include two series, known, respectively, as *Proceedings* and *Bulletin.*

The *Proceedings*, begun in 1878, is intended primarily as a medium for the publication of original papers, based on the collections of the National Museum, that set forth newly acquired facts in biology, anthropology, and geology, with descriptions of new forms and revisions of limited groups. Copies of each paper, in pamphlet form, are distributed as published to libraries and scientific organizations and to specialists and others interested in the different subjects. The dates at which these separate papers are published are recorded in the table of contents of each of the volumes.

The *Bulletin*, the first of which was issued in 1875, consists of a series of separate publications comprising monographs of large zoological groups and other general systematic treatises (occasionally in several volumes), faunal works, reports of expeditions, catalogues of type-specimens, special collections, and other material of similar nature. The majority of the volumes are octavo in size, but a quarto size has been adopted in a few instances in which large plates were regarded as indispensable. In the *Bulletin* series appear volumes under the heading *Contributions from the United States National Herbarium*, in octavo form, published by the National Museum since 1902, which contain papers relating to the botanical collections of the Museum.

The present work forms No. 136 of the *Bulletin* series.

ALEXANDER WETMORE,
Assistant Secretary, Smithsonian Institution.

WASHINGTON, D. C., March 11, 1927.

TABLE OF CONTENTS

HANDBOOK OF THE COLLECTION OF MUSICAL INSTRUMENTS IN THE UNITED STATES NATIONAL MUSEUM

Collaborator, Bureau of American Ethnology, Smithsonian Institution

INTRODUCTION

The collection of musical instruments in the United States National Museum, in its history and development, is closely associated with two interesting personalities. The founder of the collection was Dr. G. Brown Goode, Assistant Secretary of the Smithsonian Institution, in charge of the United States National Museum, who himself was an amateur musician. He included musical instruments in the classification of the branches of the Museum on its reorganization in 1879. Musical instruments were regarded by Doctor Goode as sound-emitting devices and to be grouped for exhibition by the manner in which sound was produced. To Doctor Goode's personal interest and to his scientific viewpoint the collection of musical instruments owes its start in the right direction, and it received an impetus which it has never lost.

The man most intimately connected with the present collection, however, is the late Edwin H. Hawley, who gave his best thought and strength to it from 1884 until his death in 1921. His preparation for the work consisted of two and a half years' museum work under Prof. A. E. Verrill of the Yale Peabody Museum. Previous to Mr. Hawley's time the musical instruments had been given accession numbers, but had not been classified as a separate section. He devised a system of classification based upon careful study of the classifications of similar collections in the museums of this country and Europe. This system was adopted by the Museum and forms the basis of the present work. Mr. Hawley went to the Paris Exposition in 1900, and visited London, Brussels, and other cities, in order to inspect the museums and confer with European authorities concerning the instruments needed to enrich and complete the collection in the National Museum. To this contact and subsequent correspondence may be attributed, in large measure, the remarkable completeness of the Museum collection. An exhaustive search was made for old instruments to complete synoptic series, and when these could not be obtained, copies were made from the best models.

The specimens which comprise the collection have been derived from numerous sources, some of which antedated the organization of the Smithsonian Institution. Many specimens represent an interest and cooperation on the part of other countries, rare and valuable instruments having been received as gifts from the King of Siam, Rajah Tagore, India, and other foreign potentates. Officers of the Army and Navy and consular representatives of the United States in foreign countries have obtained many musical instruments for the Museum, while other specimens have been collected by members of the staff of various branches of the Smithsonian Institution. Type specimens have been received from inventors, dealers, and manufacturers; and large numbers have been obtained from private collectors or denoted by generous individuals.

The literary material left by Mr. Hawley is extensive and has been of greatest assistance in preparing this handbook. The card index of specimens comprises 3,057 cards, with detailed information concerning each specimen. Separate card indexes were prepared by him showing the classes of musical instruments with catalogue numbers of specimens, the geographical locations whence the specimens came, the names of collectors or donors, and an index of musical terminology. The largest card index prepared by Mr. Hawley contains more than 23,000 cards, representing musical instruments in other museums or mentioned in literature, with descriptions and references. Only type specimens in the National Museum collection are included in this latter index. In addition to exhibited specimens and card indexes the musical material comprises reference books, old musical publications, photographs, and phonograph records of primitive music, some of the latter made in 1888.

The exhibit hall contains only a portion of the musical instruments, many being included in the historical or cultural material of various countries, or kept for reference in the Museum offices. The great Worch collection of pianos may be seen on the rotunda balconies of the Natural History Building.

Section 1. SOLID, SONOROUS INSTRUMENTS

GONGS

The simplest form of sonorous instrument is the gong, which may be defined as an object of stone, metal, wood, etc., struck with a mallet to produce a tone. A flat stone or a log of wood, struck in such a manner as to produce a tone, is a gong. The use of stone in

a gong ranges from the flat stones of primitive man to the beautifully carved gong of jade from Japan (Cat. No. 94890, pl. 1*d*), the
carving on the ower portion representing a bat and on the upper
an openwork design of flowers. Gongs are generally circular in
form, but a triangular metal gong was used long ago in Burma, and
a triangular stone, suspended from a wooden frame, was used in
Chinese households to announce the arrival of a guest, the number
of strokes indicating his rank. Gongs of stone and wood cut in the
shape of fish were used in Japan, and an interesting example from
China appears in this exhibit as 94858 (pl. 2*a*). The Chinese name
is literally translated as " wooden fish." The shape resembles that
of a globular sleigh bell. It is carved from a block of wood, the
loop-like handle formed by two dragons meeting nose to nose. A
five-petaled flower is carved in low relief on the sides, which is
gilded, and the body of the gong is lacquered with vermilion. It
is beaten with a round stick, the handle of which is decorated with
red cord. Another small wooden gong is in crescent form (95222).
This is suspended by a cord and beaten with a stick.

The large percussion instruments made of logs are technically
" gongs," but the term " drum " is a more convenient designation.
No. 2827 is commonly called a " war drum." It was received about
the year 1840 from the Fiji Islands and is 55 inches long and 18
inches high. It consists of a log of hard red wood, hollowed like
a trough. When in use a coil of rope forms its base. It is beaten
on the edge of the opening with two sticks, one larger than the
other, the strokes of the two alternating. Another gong made of
a log is 95157. It is not hollowed out so completely as the preceding
and is decorated with round spots burned in a row along the openings. The description says that when used in war it is beaten in
the middle, but at feasts, and the like, it is beaten between the middle
and the ends. This comes from the Gabboon River in West Africa.
A particularly interesting specimen is 174758 (pl. 3*b*) from the
Congo in Africa. It is designated as a " telegraph drum " and was
probably used by the natives in conveying rhythmic messages. It is
made from a solid log and has two holes drilled through from one
side to within half an inch of the other side; a slot 1 inch wide
and 10 inches long connects these and is drilled to the same depth.
The cavity inside the drum was made by working from the holes
and an opening in each end. Not all the wood is excavated, but a coni-
cal-shaped chunk, divided by the slot, is left attached to the front
side. The outside is ornamented with curved lines. From each end
projects an ear, and in these are inserted the ends of a stick bent
in a half circle. This crude article has an air of mystery and suggests the wild, primitive environment from whence it came.

A comparatively small wooden gong from the Samoan Islands is 152749. It is made of a rounded block of wood and the ends slope like the bow and stern of a canoe. An oblong opening is cut in the upper side. The drumstick is a conical piece of dark red wood. A flat wooden gong from China is 94856.

Gongs of bamboo are commonly used in Asiatic countries. No. 95,619 (pl. 3d) is a bamboo gong open at one end that was sounded by striking the sides with a stick or by holding it vertically and striking the closed end on the ground. Another bamboo gong (54190, pl. 3c) is called a "watchman's rattle" and was received from China in 1876. A Chinese priest's gong of bamboo is 54156 (pl. 3a).

The metal gong varies from small disks of hammered bell metal to huge gongs with surface elaborately damascened. It is said that the metal gong was used in China a little later than the time of Confucius (478 B. C.) and that it was the first metal instrument introduced into Japan. Its antiquity in Egypt, Africa, India, and the Malayan Islands will remain a matter of conjecture. The uses of the metal gongs are varied and interesting. A Chinese gong was carried by servants before a Mandarin in his sedan to give notice of his approach, a certain number of strokes at intervals indicating his rank; a gong was also carried in processions and beaten to drive away evil spirits. During eclipses it was beaten to frighten the heavenly dog as he was about to devour the moon. In Japan "a kind of gong was suspended before idols and struck by worshippers to arouse the attention of the god." In both countries it accompanied the wedding and funeral processions, and also served the purpose of a clock. The soldiers on guard at night were accustomed to sound the large divisions of the night on a drum, and the lesser divisions on a gong. In India the gong was beaten in the temple at the hour of ceremony or sacrifice, and in Burma the gong went forth with the warriors, its sound being heard in battle at a distance of 4 or 5 miles. From Burma we have a flat, somewhat thick plate of metal resembling the outline of a hat with a turned up brim (95497). This was suspended by a cord in Buddhist temples and struck with a wooden mallet to call the god's attention to the offerings.

A common form of Chinese gong consists of a thin round plate with the edges turned up, like a shallow sieve or tambourine. It is held in the left hand by a cord and struck with a stick held in the right hand, this stick having a large padded knob at the end. Several excellent examples of these gongs are in the collection. The metal may be brass, but is usually an alloy of 80 parts copper to 20 parts of tin. It is a remarkable property of the alloys of copper and tin that they become malleable by being heated and then plunged into cold water. Gongs are thus treated after being cast and are then hammered. The marks of the hammer can be seen on the exhibited specimens. This process was a secret in Europe until found out some years ago by M. d'Arect, a French chemist.

A typical Siamese gong is 3992 (pl. 1e), which was a gift from the King of Siam to President Pierce in 1857. A chinese priest's gong is shown as 94860. The gong is shaped like a tea plate and it is suspended by three short cords in a round frame with a handle. It is struck with two slender bamboo wands having heads of bone. A " gong harmonium " was used by Buddhist priests in funeral ceremonies. The specimen exhibited (94848) consists of an open wooden frame divided by cross-bars into nine squares. In these squares are suspended nine round gongs, each having a different pitch. They are struck with a slender elastic bamboo having a dice-shaped bone head.

A " shark's mouth gong " from Japan (96632) was obtained through the courtesy of Mrs. J. Crosby Brown. It is ornamented on the center of one side with a nine-petaled chrysanthemum surrounded by three raised concentric circles. On the opposite side the flower is replaced by the five drums of " Rarden," the thunder god. This little gong was hung at the entrance to a shrine and struck by worshippers to attract the attention of the god. A peculiar Chinese gong is 94859 (pl. 2e). When in use it is probably held with the opening upward, like a bowl.

The collection contains several of the flat gongs with upturned edges which are used in Malay countries. An interesting example is 94917, made of hammered bronze, which was collected in 1891 by R. Wildemann, United States Consul at Singapore. A majority of the gongs now used in the Philippine Islands are of Chinese manufacture, but in former times the flat gongs were beaten from native copper. A Filipino dancer holds the gong in his left hand by a loop of cord and pounds it with a stick. The writer heard this type of gong used by the Igorot at the Louisiana Purchase Exposition in St. Louis in 1904 and noted that the tone produced by striking the gong near the edge was approximately a major third higher than when it was struck in the middle. These two tones, interspersed with rests, were combined in various rhythms. In an Igorot village the writer saw the flat gong held on the player's knees and struck alternately with a stick and with the palm of the hand.

A notable specimen of this type is 95204 (pl. 1c), from Korea. A small pair of Chinese gongs are only 5¾ inches in diameter (54018). They are of bell metal, unpolished, and were suspended by a cord. An elaborate gong from Calcutta is 92721 (pl. 1g), ornamented with designs which are made by scraping through the dark oxide of the surface. This specimen is of hammered bell metal. Two Chinese gongs are 54080 and 54017 and a specimen from Singapore is 94917.

A particularly fine gong was given to President Pierce in 1856 by the King of Siam (3991, pl. 2b). The shell and head are of beaten brass or bell metal, in one piece. The single head is flat and ornamented with designs in repoussé. On the border of the head are four metal frogs in full relief, placed an equal distance apart. The two drumsticks are of rosewood, their lower ends tipped with ivory ferrules. Their heads are cylindrical and tapering, and covered with a network of white cord.

A Chinese gong rests on a carved wood base with five legs (84891, pl. 2d). This is of bronze cast in one piece and was collected in 1891 by Dr. Julius Neumann.

A different sort of gong, common in Malay countries, has a knob, or " boss," from which the sides slope sharply to their widest diameter, then turn inward to a slighly smaller diameter. Such gongs range from 4 or 5 inches in diameter and about 3 inches in depth, to huge gongs that are about 20 inches in diameter and almost the same in depth. This type is probably Chinese in origin, and is frequently used in series of 8 or 10, graduated in size, and placed on cords which are strung the length of a wooden frame, near the ground, with the smallest at the player's left hand (312855, pl. 2c). The performer sits on the ground beside the frame, holds a padded stick in each hand, and uses both sticks in striking the tops of the gongs. It is said that a very large gong is sometimes hung near a series of small gongs to provide the lowest tone, but the large gong is used chiefly in transmitting messages. Such a gong is struck on top of the boss, and the player's left hand is placed around the boss in such a manner as to affect the sound. There is ample evidence of the accuracy with which messages are thus transmitted, but it appears that the method has not been studied in detail.

A Siamese " gong harmonium " from Bangkok was exhibited at the Centennial Exposition in 1876 and, with a large collection, was presented to this Museum by the King of Siam (27316, pl. 4). It comprises 16 gongs, and is exhibited with a figure showing the manner in which it was played.

A curious instrument classified as a " multiple gong " resembles a bundle of bamboo rods wrapped in matting (152744). This was collected in Samoa or Navigator Islands by Harold M. Sewall and described as follows by Mr. Hawley:

The mat is straightened out. The 15 bamboo sticks are laid in two rows, commencing with the largest at one end of the mat, and extend past its middle, the inner ends of the two rows passing by each other. The mat is rolled, inclosing the bamboos, quite tightly and tied with a string. It is beaten with three sticks from which the bark has been removed. Used at their night dances.

BELLS

The bell differs from the gong in being deeper and usually having a clapper suspended inside it. It may be suspended or held in the hand and swung to and fro, the sound being produced by the clapper striking the inside of the bell, or it may be in a fixed position and sounded by the striking of a hammer on its external or its internal surface.

More intimately than any other instrument the bell is associated with the joys and sorrows of mankind. It has rung for weddings and funerals, given alarm of danger, and, in scenes of peace, been heard as the cattle bell. The jester's cap was trimmed with bells, and in the ancient synagogue the high priest's robe was edged with golden bells. In Egypt the feast of Osiris was announced by the ringing of bells and throughout the Christian world the bell is rung as a call to worship. The Roman Catholic church uses it in the solemn service of the Mass. Bells are used in the modern orchestra, and for this purpose they are tubular in shape, several being hung on a frame.

Bells were used in ancient Greece, Rome, and Persia, while China and Japan have bells of great antiquity. In ancient times the Chinese used a bell for the same purpose that we use a tuning fork; a bell also served as a measure of weight in business transactions, a special bell being kept in the temple as a standard. Bronze bells have been found in Assyria, and a small bell was found in a mummy case in Egypt.

From Africa come little bells made of nutshells, and from Siam are bells of bamboo which were tied around the necks of elephants when they were turned into the jungle to graze at night. The Hopi Indians made bells of the horn of mountain sheep and the Zuni made bells of pottery. Silver, gold, brass, copper, iron, and bronze have also been used in the making of bells.

A typical bell is shaped like an inverted cup with slightly flaring edge and, as indicated, usually has a clapper suspended and swinging freely. The earliest bells were often four-sided, made of thin plates of metal riveted together; others were cone shaped and some of the latter were in pairs known as " double bells." One such pair (95220, pl. 5f) was used by an African chief when he approached a village to announce his visit, which was not always welcome to the people.

A particularly interesting set of native bells is from Java (95661, pl. 6a, two only). This set consists of four frames of graduated sizes, each formed of a long strip of split bamboo bent in a half circle at its middle, with the ends parallel and fastened to a base.

In each frame three bells of bamboo are suspended. When the frame is swung from side to side the striking of studs against the square holes in the base causes the bells in the frame to sound. It is said that each set gives a fundamental tone with its first and second octave; each set of bells is held by a different player, and the tones of the melody are sounded one after another by the proper player swinging his frame of bells. The effect is said to be very pleasing to the ear.

The metal hand bell probably preceded the bell which was suspended, indeed the bells were comparatively small until the thirteenth century. The earliest attempt at bell music seems to have consisted in striking a row of small bells with a hammer held in the hand, and illustrations on manuscripts of the twelfth or thirteenth century show this manner of playing upon 3, 4, or 8 bells. In the religious fervor of the Middle Ages these sets of bells were made larger, hung in towers, and rung by means of ropes. Such sets averaged about 10 bells and were known as chimes. From these were developed the carillon, which prospered especially in the flat countries of Belgium and Holland where they could be heard a long distance. The carillon at Ghent contains 52 bells and several other old carillon have more than 40 bells on which music in two or three parts can be played. The recent development of the carillon is of importance, there being 187 carillons in existence at the present time (1925), many of which are in the United States. England, for many centuries, has been famous for its bell foundries, and the finest carillons are now made in that country. By its tuning in "equal temperament" as well as by its extended compass the carillon has taken its place among accurate musical instruments. The importance of a carillon depends upon the size of its lowest bell, the largest existing carillon bell being 98 inches in diameter, weighing 20,720 pounds, and giving the tone E below middle C. One bell is provided for each half tone of the diatonic scale, the number ranging from 23 to 53 bells, set in vibration by a keyboard and elaborate connecting mechanism.

Metal is such an enduring substance that many bells have come down to us from antiquity, giving forth the same sound as of old but unable to tell us their history. Thus a certain bronze bell bears a procession of warriors in low relief, an elephant bearing trophies, and a prisoner walking beside it. A story of triumph is recorded in the metal but still is veiled in mystery.

The bell once used by a Buddhist priest (96633, pl. 5d) is ornamented with animals, and its handle is the figure of a double-faced god. Among other hand bells exhibited is 95623 (pl. 5i), from Korea, which represents a bud showing five petals. A loop is cast in the crown of the bell from which a forged iron clapper is swung by a wire link. No. 94862 (pl. 5a), from China, is a small cast bronze bell with a cast handle, like a dinner bell; the tongue is rough finished and left blackened. A "wind bell" from Korea is of cast brass (151616, pl. 5c). From the clapper is suspended a fish cast from brass almost as thin as paper. Such a bell is hung from the eaves at each of the four corners of a temple.

An interesting war bell of wrought iron from West Africa is 174751 (pl. 5j). The curious bell with a curved handle (95221, pl. 5k) is from the French Congo, and was collected by Carl Steckleman.

Concerning the use of the bell in India, Capt. Meadows Taylor says:

No ceremony of sacrifice or oblation is performed without the preliminary tinkling of the bell, which is repeated at certain intervals during the ritual. . . . There can be no doubt that the practice of using it is as ancient as Hinduism itself, and the rituals, liturgies, and works of ceremonial observance define the use to be made of it. By Mohammedans the use of a bell in any form that I am aware of is unknown.

No. 92722 (pl. 5h) is from India and has a bell-shaped body with a cast handle. On top of the handle is the figure of a kneeling winged god. The bell is of hammered bell metal, the outside turned and polished, the inside is rough as it came from the mold. A Chinese priest's bell at the end of a rod (94863) has no clapper and was probably sounded by striking against some object.

The use of pottery in making bells is shown by 214482 (pl. 5e), which is made of red earthenware, decorated with three stripes of white. It has a ball of pottery suspended as a clapper, and came from Italy.

A curious little Shinto bell from Japan is 96634 (pl. 5g), made of hammered and polished brass. Inclosed are two small fragments of brass that serve as a clapper. Somewhat larger is a dog bell, used when hunting (174750). This is made of a heart-shaped nutshell decorated with four lines of white clay. The apex is pierced for a cord and an opening is cut in the lower end. It was collected in Bongola, West Africa, and obtained from Hon. Dorsey Mohun, of the United States Department of State.

Attention is directed to the large suspended bell (4329, pl. 5b), which was collected by Commodore M. C. Perry on his expedition to Japan in 1852–1854, and presented by him to the museum. It is of cast bell metal with cylindrical body and conoidal top. The four squares each contain 12 raised knobs, which are supposed to represent the snails that crawled on the head of Buddha and prevented a sunstroke. From the apex of the bell project two dragon's heads, united by the double trident-shaped "precious jewel," forming a loop by which the bell is suspended. This type of bell was struck over the circular boss near the mouth with a swinging beam of wood.

The Japanese temple bell (94631, pl. 7*b*) is of beaten bronze hung in a frame of carved teakwood. On its surface may be seen the small protuberances said to represent snails. The beater is of varnished red wood with head of kid stuffed with raw silk. This bell is extremely sonorous and was used in religious services. It was collected in 1884 by the United States diplomatic representative at Tokio.

A particularly interesting bell is 94961 (pl. 7*a*), collected by Dr. Julius Neumann, in Canton, China. This bell is suspended in a manner that passed out of use before 1279. According to Engel, the Chinese at an early period had "a somewhat square bell made of an alloy of 1 lb. of tin to 6 of copper." It is said that "the first alterations were made in the Sung dynasty, when the ring at the side of the handle was moved to the top, so the bell hung straight instead of obliquely."[1] The Sung dynasty ruled from 960 to 1279 A. D. A second peculiarity of this bell is that the mouth is not straight across but rises from the ends to the middle, forming an obtuse angle on both sides. The material of the bell is cut bronze, and on each of its four sides are twisted cones, representing the snails that protected the head of Buddha.

A different type of bell, also suspended in a carved frame, is 94962 (pl. 7*c*). On the outside are four diagrams, suggesting astronomical charts, showing stars connected by raised lines. It was struck with a small wooden mallet. A Chinese bell of cast metal with a ring handle is 5390. The history of this bell is not recorded.

CYMBALS

As seen in a modern orchestra, the cymbals are not conspicuous instruments, but they have a particularly interesting history. They are a pair of round, thin metal plates with a leather strap through the center of each, by which the performer holds it in his hand. The metal is usually an alloy of 80 parts copper to 20 of tin skillfully hammered by hand. To produce a good tone they are not struck together but rubbed against each other in a single sliding motion. If one cymbal is used alone and struck with a padded stick, it becomes a gong. Wagner introduces this in single notes in "Die Walkure," producing a remarkable effect.

The gong had its origin in a pounding on stones or logs by uncivilized peoples, but the cymbal is an instrument of dignity, associated with the highest culture of the ancient world. According to Xenophon, the cymbal was invented by Cybele and used at her feasts in 1580 B. C. Cymbals are represented in the sculptures of Nimroud and were used in religious and patriotic observances

---

[1] North China Branch, Royal Asiatic Society, 1908, p. 40.

by the Egyptians, Assyrians, Jews, Etrurians, Greeks, and Romans. It is interesting to note that a pair of cymbals were found in the coffin inclosing the mummy of Ankhape, a sacred musician of ancient Egypt.

In the earlier books of the Old Testament cymbals are frequently mentioned among the musical instruments used in the temple. Dr. I. M. Casanowicz, Assistant Curator, Division of Old World Archeology, United States National Museum, says that:

> The cymbals were of two kinds. One consisted of two large plates of metal with wide flat rims, and were played by being strapped to the hands and clashed together. The others were conical, or cuplike, with thin edges, and were played by bringing down the one sharply on the other while held stationary, eliciting a high-pitched note.[2]

Turkish cymbals are considered of the finest quality, and the collection includes such a pair (72878) obtained from J. Howard Foote in 1883. These were made in Constantinople and are 12½ inches in diameter. A pair of Chinese cymbals of about the same size are of bronze (94857), and examples of Chinese cymbals of hammered bell metal are shown as 54018 and 94852 (pl. 1f). The Burmese cymbals (95486) are of heavy hammered bell metal in the shape of a disk with bossed center. A smaller pair from Korea (95208) are of bronze, turned inside and outside, and having the outer surface polished. A small pair of Burmese cymbals are 95486 (pl. 1b).

A curious pair of iron cymbals (125560) is from the Soudan. Each consists of two disks connected by a broad crossbar. The Spanish cymbals with red tassels 95563 (pl. 1a), were collected by Dr. Walter Hough of the United States National Museum.

CASTANETS

The castanet is commonly associated with pleasure and picturesque dancing, as the cymbal is associated with pomp and dignity. The name is Spanish and originated, it is supposed, from the fact that castanets were made from the wood of the chestnut tree, "Castana." The materials include wood, shell, brass, bronze, and iron. Castanets, like cymbals, are played in pairs, but they differ from cymbals in being so small that a player holds one pair in each hand. According to Mahillon, the Spanish dancers use two sizes, a treble and a bass. "The smaller pair, which they call the female, is held in the right hand and used to mark the rhythm. The larger, which they call the male, is held in the left hand and marks the fundamental notes."

There are many shapes of castanets. Two common types are (1) small disks of wood or metal having a boss at their centers, the

---

[2] Annual Report, Smithsonian Institution, 1922, p. 487.

center of this boss being pierced with a hole for the cord by which the disk is attached to the player's finger, and (2) a pair of somewhat oval pieces of wood or metal, hinged together by one of the long sides; one pair is held in each hand and they are clashed together by the opening and closing of the player's hand.

An interesting pair of Syrian castanets (95145) was obtained by Erhard Bissinger, United States consul at Beirut. These have scalloped edges and the outer surface is engraved. A pair of Egyptian castanets (95174) is made of brass or bronze. Among the specimens of this instrument is 95496, a Burmese castanet only 1⅜ inches in diameter. Concerning their use it is said that "one castanet is held tightly by the thumb and forefinger, the other loosely between forefinger and second finger. They are made to strike each other by a movement of the wrist."

RATTLES

Many musical instruments of uncivilized peoples have a counterpart in the music of civilization, but the rattle is an exception. The rattle remains the musical instrument of primitive man. More than any other instrument it is associated with the working of magic, and among the American Indians it is often used in the treatment of the sick. According to J. R. Swanton: [3]

The rattle was generally regarded as a sacred object, not to be brought forth on ordinary occasions but confined to rituals, religious feasts, shamanastic performances, etc. This character is emphasized in the sign language of the plains, where the sign for rattle is the basis of all signs indicating that which is sacred.

Rattles were held in the hand, fastened to the clothing, or made into necklaces or anklets in such a manner as to make a noise with every movement of the wearer. Perhaps no musical instrument gives such opportunity for decoration as the rattle, and in this, as in the material of the rattle itself, we see the effective use of materials which were easily obtained.

E. H. Hawley divided rattles into four classes: Rattles, clappers, notched sticks, and sistra, saying:

The first class consists of hollow bodies inclosing loose balls, pebbles, seeds, etc., or hollow or sonorous bodies so arranged as to strike one another. These are made of wood, fruit shells, basket work, metal, raw hide, etc. The second class has two or more sticks rattled together, as often seen in negro minstrel troupes, and the clappers of the North Pacific coast. These may be made of bone, wood, metal, etc. The simplest of the third class consists of a stick having transverse notches or grooves made across its face, this face being rubbed by a bone or stick. In this class are included those rattles which have a toothed wheel so constructed that when revolved the teeth raise springs and suddenly release them, also similar ones in which the wheel is stationary and

---

[3] Handbook of American Indians, Bulletin 30, Bureau American Ethnology, p. 355.

the springs are made to revolve around it. The fourth class comprises all rattles of the ancient sistrum form, also those in which the loose bars are replaced by jingles.

A hollow object containing loose, smaller objects is the typical rattle of all primitive people and, as indicated, is the first division of the first class of rattles according to the present grouping. A characteristic rattle of British Guiana consists of a large bamboo tube containing nutshells or fruit pits. Other rattles were made of several small bamboo reeds, bound together with fiber and partially filled with seeds. In Africa dried fruit shells were used as rattles, the inclosed seeds making a sound. Rattles made of pottery have come to us from the Aztecs in the form of seated or standing figures of grotesque outline with broad flat heads. These vessels contain tiny bits of clay which rattle when they are shaken.

A rattle familiar in the southwest is made of a gourd containing pebbles or clay pellets. An excellent example from the Sia of New Mexico collected by James Stevenson is 134189 (pl. 8d), a smaller from Walpi is 68737, and a painted gourd rattle of the Zuni is 286073, while 175626 (pl. 8h) is a decorated gourd rattle from the Arapaho collected by James Mooney. No. 272591 is from South Darien, Panama, the gourd inclosing canna seeds. A ceremonial rattle of the Oneida is made of the entire body of a turtle (248712, pl. 8f). Stiff rawhide is used for this type of rattle by the Plains tribes, and a cylindrical box made of birch bark is used by the Chippewa Indians in ceremonies of the Grand Medicine Society (263230). Small receptacles containing tiny pebbles are often attached to the clothing or body of a dancer. Such an ornament made of cocoons (324885) is from the Seri Indians of Mexico.

The characteristic rattle of Indians living in Alaska and British Columbia is carved of wood. The rattle is made in two longitudinal sections, each hollowed on one side to form a receptacle for the pebbles and carved on the other side. These sections are usually tied together with thongs to form the rattle. Such a rattle collected at Port Simpson, British Columbia, by Swan is carved on one side with a human mask held by a bear (20585, pl. 8g). The two sections are tied together at the edges and nailed together at the handle. A large specimen is 229544 (pl. 8e). An interesting rattle, carved in a manner typical of the Northwest coast, is 316756 (pl. 8a), collected by Sheldon Jackson. A Tlingit rattle collected by Lieut. F. M. Ring, United States Army, in 1869, is carved in the form of a bird and has five tufts of human hair fastened to each wing (9106, pl. 8c). All these are described as " Shaman's rattle."

The second division of this class of rattles comprises " hollow or sonorous bodies so arranged as to strike one another." Nutshells, as well as fruit pits and small brown shells, were strung on a fiber cord by the natives of Melanesia and similar countries. An interesting specimen (21328) from the Hupa Indians of California was collected in 1875 by Stephen Powers. It consists of 37 deer hoofs attached to buckskin thongs. The writer saw a similar rattle used at the cremation of a Yuma Indian in 1922. A Yaqui dancing belt from Sonora, Mexico, is 129850. The large variety of materials used in this type of rattle includes the " dewclaws " of the deer, the beaks of ptarmigan and puffin, the claws of the bear, the shells of small turtles, and the flat pecten shells of the Northwest coast. From the Makah of Cape Flattery there is a doctor's rattle of pecten shells on a hoop of whalebone. (328602, pl. 8b). A pair of Tlingit rattles (20786, pl. 8i) was collected by J. G. Swan in 1875. These consist of goat hoofs at the end of sticks which were held in each hand. Somewhat similar rattles are common among the Plains tribes, such as a rattle consisting of a wand covered with leather to which are attached triangular pieces of deer hoof.

The second class of rattles consists of " bones " or clappers. Such instruments are in use in the Far East and were possibly used in Africa, as they are one of the principal instruments used by negro minstrels. In England they were known in the seventeenth century as " knicky knackers." Shakespeare mentions them as follows: " Bottom, I have a reasonable good ear for music, let us have the tongs and bones." [4] Originally they were sections of a rib of an ox and that material is still used. When made of hard wood they have the form of such sections. The player holds a pair of " bones " in each hand. One is held rigidly between the first finger and the ball of the thumb, the other is held loosely between the second and third fingers. Like the castanets, they can be clicked together in simple strokes or in rapidly succeeding strokes forming varied rhythms. The sound is much louder than that of the castanets. An instrument of hard wood like the " bones " of the negro minstrels has been noted in southern India, and an interesting set of three clappers from China is exhibited (54187). The Greeks used shells or bits of pottery in the manner of clappers to mark the rhythm of the dance while the flute played the melody. A type of clapper more widely distributed than the pair of bones consists of a piece of bamboo split at one end. Such a clapper (or " slapstick ") used in the Philippines consists of a piece of bamboo split a portion of its length and having the prongs pointed like corn leaves (235154, pl. 8k). It is said that " during the earlier months of the year a Benguet Igorot woman will not go on the trail without carrying one of these instruments. It is carried in the left hand and made to

---

[4] Midsummer's Night's Dream, act 4, scene 1.

strike against the right wrist." A typical Dyak instrument is longer and split into four prongs or sections at one end.

A clapper used in Ireland was made of small plates of brass or shingles of wood, the French used a clapper with their ancient dances, and the Latin people to the south used it to mark the rhythm of dancing in the worship of Cybele.

The clapper used by the Indians of Alaska and British Columbia is often carved and painted somewhat similarly to the rattles. The writer was informed that a clapper of this sort was used by medicine men who struck it against the body of the patient during their treatment. An example of this instrument from the Tlingit Indians of Alaska (16285, pl. 8*j*) is described as follows by Mr. Hawley:

Dance rattle or clapper carved from wood in the shape of a short, thick paddle, split longitudinally for part of its length. One section is solid with the part which forms the handle, the other is hinged to the handle with a whale bone spring. The flat (inner) surface of each section is hollowed out like a spoon.

The third class of rattle is known as the notched stick rattle. This consists of two parts, a stick (or other substance) having notches cut across its face, and a shorter stick (or other substance) that is rubbed across the notches. A resonator is sometimes used to amplify the sound. A typical instrument consists of a stick about 1 inch in diameter and 20 to 25 inches long, cut with equidistant notches on one side for about two-thirds its length, and rasped with a stick or bone about 6 inches long. Resonators vary with the locality.

The history and distribution of this instrument are particularly interesting. The earliest example, so far as known, is the Chinese ÿu, which was used in the Confucian ceremonies and occupied a position of prominence on the west side of the temple. It is of hollow carved wood in the form of a crouching tiger on a rectangular box. On the back of the tiger are 27 teeth, resembling a saw. At the close of each verse in the temple songs the tiger is struck three times on the head with a beater made of split bamboo which is rapidly passed over the projections on the back, producing a rasping sound. In Japan a similar instrument is called " gyo." Evidence of the use of human bones in the making of this instrument have been unearthed in Mexico. A primitive example of this rattle is 231000 (pl. 9*e*), consisting of the lower jaw (mandible) of a horse. This was used by negro slaves and formerly by negro minstrels. A stick was rubbed across the teeth, and at the same time the instrument was used as a gong. It is said that:

The Christy minstrels held the instrument at the point of the jaw by the left hand, the stick or beater was held in the right hand between the cheek bones, striking one cheek bone for a single beat and both for a double beat.

There was also a varying pitch of the sound according to the point struck, the sharper sounds if struck near the teeth and the lower one if struck near the joint over which the jaw was hinged. Occasionally the beater was rubbed across the teeth like a notched stick rattle.

Among the Ute Indians several notched stick rattles are used as an accompaniment to the bear dance, held in the spring when the bear comes from its hibernation. The ends of the notched sticks are rested upon a large piece of zinc which covers a hole in the ground known as the bear's cave. This hole or trench acts as a resonator. A typical example of an old bear dance rattle is 211004 (pl. 9b), in which the notched stick is shaped like the jawbone of a bear and the "rubber" is a stout bone. The notched stick is held in a position similar to that of a violincello, and the player kneels behind it as he draws the "rubber" up and down the notches, sharply accenting the downward motion. The resultant sound is said to be like the growling of a bear. The instrument is commonly known by the Spanish term "morache." At the present time a straight stick is used, with a short stout stick as a "rubber," and (except in the bear dance) a shallow basket, inverted on the ground, is used as a resonator. Painted and decorated rattles of this type are used by the Hopi and Zuñi. Among the Yaqui in Arizona the writer saw a notched stick rattle used at a deer dance. The notched stick was the "rib" of the sahauro cactus, the "rubber" was a slender stick of greasewood, and the resonator was half a gourd, inverted on the ground. A similar instrument from the Papago, probably made of mesquite wood, is 317605 (pl. 9i).

A gourd shell, having notches cut through the outer skin is 301527 from Porto Rico. This was probably rasped with a stick. The Museum collection contains specimens of this rattle from the Zuni, Hopi, Piute, and Maya Indians, and an interesting specimen from Guatemala in which the notches are not equidistant but in groups of three or four.

A sound similar to that of a notched stick rattle is produced by revolving a wooden spring against a toothed cylinder. Such an instrument is described as a "revolving rattle." An example of this instrument is 238056 (pl. 9a) from the Philippine Islands, commonly called by the Spanish term "matracca." The body of the instrument revolves around the handle, making a loud, rasping sound. The instrument is used to frighten locusts away from the cultivated fields.

The fourth class of rattle is the sistrum, commonly called the "jingling johnny." This is found in many forms, in many countries, both ancient and modern. Briefly described, it consists of a frame, to which are attached small objects that jingle when the frame is shaken. The word "frame," as here used, includes a wide variety of objects, such as rings, bent rods, crescents, balls, hollow domes, and flat, spoon-shaped objects, while the materials attached thereto include small bells, brass disks, loose bent rods, coins, short chains, and metal bars. A familiar example is a "baby's rattle" with jingling attachments. One description of the sistrum states that it is "the national instrument of Turkey and consists of a brass frame with numerous bells, carried on a long perpendicular pole, the point of which is surmounted by a crescent and the well-known streamer of horsehair. It is used in military or "janissary music." Two specimens from Turkey are shown in this collection and described as follows:

The "Turkish Crescent" (95314, pl. 9c) is a hollow crescent-shaped body made of sheet brass, its lower edge strung with small conical bells. It has an iron staff fitting loosely in a hollow wood and brass handle. It was carried upright and jolted up and down, and according to Mahillon it was introduced into European military bands about the beginning of the nineteenth century. It is interesting to note that the Irish, in old times, had an instrument very similar to the Turkish crescent, known as the "musical branch," and consisting of a bent rod adorned with numerous bells.

Somewhat similar is the "Turkish hat" or "jingling johnny." (95315, pl. 9d.) Three hat-shaped domes of brass of graduated sizes are placed one above the other on an iron staff running through their centers. The staff is surmounted by a crescent. To the edges of each dome are suspended small bells, 9 on the lowest and 7 on the middle one and 5 on the upper one, with the same number of globular bells alternating with the others. The iron staff fits loosely in a wooden handle so that it can be jolted up and down.

No. 96450 (pl. 9f) is a ceremonial spearhead from Ceylon. It is a hollow conical piece of wrought iron decorated with three fluted rings. The middle ring is loose and makes a noise when the spear is shaken. A cluster of hollow bell-shaped objects forms a sistrum rattle from Korea (95620). They have no balls inside but sound by striking against each other.

In ancient Egypt the sistrum "was chiefly used by females in religious performances" and was associated with the worship of Isis. An Egyptian instrument of this type is called a Dervish rattle, as it is carried by the dervishes in their religious dances. An excellent example of the dervish rattle is 95199 (pl. 9g), which comes from Cairo and consists of an iron rod 20¾ inches long, its upper end driven into a spherical wooden ball of heavy wood. The ball is studded with brass-headed nails and from its greatest diameter are hung 11 short chains, each with a metal pendant. A sistrum rattle from Africa has small rings of brass or iron wire depending from a flat piece of metal, and similar rattles from Korea have jingling, globular bells. These are not exhibited in this collection.

Among the Yaqui Indians of Arizona the writer saw a rattle similar to 9394 (pl. 9*h*) used in the deer dance. It was not shaken aloft in the usual manner. The dancer's arm hung at his side and the rattle in his hand was shaken lightly as he danced.

VIBRATING BARS

Many centuries ago a bar of wood or metal was suspended and struck with a mallet, after the manner of a bell or gong. Although a bar of wood or metal is more primitive than a gong or bell, its practical use, so far as recorded, does not appear to be any more ancient than these instruments.

When Saladin, the Turkish emperor, conquered Jerusalem he commanded that all the bells, great and small, should be broken in order to remove the means of calling the people together. This was also done in Greece and other conquered countries, after which the Greeks used bars of wood or iron in place of bells. One bar of this sort was 90 inches long, 18 inches wide, and 3 inches thick, and was attached to a tower with iron chains and struck with a heavy hammer. Bells are not allowed in Mohammedan countries (according to the Century Dictionary), so bars of wood or metal are used to summon worshippers. A bar of iron was used like a bell in the Greek Church as late as the eighteenth century.

A specimen of metal bar and beater (1125) was obtained by Lieut. C. Ringgold, United States Navy, on the northwest coast of the United States, on the "Exploring Expedition of Wilkes," dated 1838–1842. The bar and beater are both of polished steel, the former with one end flattened and perforated, possibly for a cord to suspend it, the latter of the same diameter and slightly longer.

We can readily understand how the "musical bar" was bent to form the triangle (55756). This instrument made its appearance in the Middle Ages and at that time it was about the same shape as the present instrument, but had some ornamentation on the metal. In the seventeenth century this instrument was used by the Turkish janissaries, or militia. Each company of janissaries had a musician at its head, and the military band organized in this connection had two triangles among its instruments.[5] The triangle is frequently used in modern orchestral music for brilliant and sparkling effects.

A modern xylophone consists of a number of vibrating bars of wood or metal, producing different gradations of pitch, placed side by side according to their sequence of pitch and struck with one or more hammers. This instrument is familiar to musicians.

---

[5] Mahillon, vol. 2, p. 189.

The oriental form of xlyophone has a rectangular box which serves as a resonator for all the vibrating bars. In the collection are 96841, a Japanese xylophone having 16 bars of hard redwood, and 95491 (pl. 10b), a Burmese instrument with 25 bars of bamboo of graduated sizes. The latter instrument was played at marriages, at the boring of children's ears, and for the entertainment of Burmese kings before retiring. Two Siamese xylophones were presented to the Museum in 1876 by the King of Siam. The treble instrument (27321, pl. 10c) has 22 bars of bamboo. The corresponding bass instrument (27320) is longer and has 17 bars of bamboo, longer and heavier than in the treble instrument. With these is shown a very small instrument of the same type (96581, pl. 10a), collected in Lower Siam by Dr. W. L. Abbott in 1896. The vibrating bars are of iron, and Doctor Abbott writes that sometimes only one such strip of iron is used.

The marimba may be described as a xylophone with a resonator under each bar. A crude form of this instrument was used in Africa as early as the seventeenth century. Later it was introduced into Mexico and Central America, and has its highest development in Guatemala. The African instrument consisted of a rectangular frame with vibrating bars and gourd resonators which could be placed on the ground or slung from the player's shoulders in such a manner as to hang horizontally in front of him. These instruments were often played together, and Livingston, when in Africa, saw a quartette of marimba combined with three drums.

Two particularly fine examples of the African marimba are exhibited. No. 93876 is from Senegambia. The four side rails of the frame are strips of bamboo, and the ends are of dark redwood. Thongs are passed back and forth on this frame, supporting 14 sounding bars of hard redwood. Beneath each bar, but not touching it, is a gourd. These vary in size to correspond with the length of the sounding bar. Each gourd has an opening in the top and also a small hole in the side. Over this hole is stretched a piece of the cocoon of some silk-spinning caterpillar. The instrument was carried by a belt over the player's shoulders and struck with two drumsticks having India rubber heads. A similar instrument from Liberia is 43071 (pl. 11a), a gift from John H. Smyth, who was United States minister to that country in 1880. This marimba has 15 sounding bars resting on twisted ropes of rawhide and held in place by smaller rawhide thongs. The spherical gourd resonators vary in diameter from 2½ to 6 inches, and as in the preceding instrument, each gourd has an opening upward toward the corresponding bar, and an opening at the side, which is covered with a piece of wild cocoon.

The marimba used in Central America consists of a topless table, trapezoidal in shape, having cords stretched its length. These cords support bars of wood, graduated in size, and beneath each is suspended a resonator. The instrument is played by four or five performers, each using a pair of drumsticks. A flexible wood is used for these sticks, and at the end of each is a flat round head made of strips of raw rubber. The sticks vary in size and weight, the smaller bars being struck with lighter sticks. A marimba from Guatemala (15248, pl. 11b) was made by the Tactic natives and given to the Museum by Henry Hague in 1874. The frame is 67⅝ inches long and it has 22 bars of sonorous wood graduated in length from 9 to 14 inches. Long cylindrical gourds are placed beneath the bars as resonators, and each has an aperture in its side, over which is placed a round lump of wax or pitch, pierced with $\frac{3}{16}$-inch hole. The striking sticks are with the instrument.

Wooden resonators are commonly used in this instrument. A group of players on such a marimba is shown in Plate 12.

A xylophone from Java (95663, pl. 6b) is composed of 12 sections of bamboo, of graduated lengths and diameters, each having one end closed by a joint. These are placed side by side and fastened with cords. It is supposed this instrument was suspended from the ceiling and struck with slender sticks.

VIBRATING TONGUES

The form of this class of instruments most familiar to a musician of the white race is the tuning fork; the form most familiar to the student of oriental music is the zanze. The music box is also in this class.

Tuning forks were invented about the middle of the eighteenth century by John Shore, Handel's famous trumpeter. They are usually made of tempered steel, their tone is comparatively free from upper partial tones ("overtones") and their pitch is not disturbed by ordinary changes of temperature. They are tuned by filing the ends of the prongs to raise the pitch, and by filing the base between the prongs to lower the pitch. The manner of use is too familiar to need description. A series of tuning forks of graduations of pitch is exhibited (261050). These were made in Japan.

The zanze is an African instrument consisting of bamboo or metal tongues fastened near one end to a small board and twanged with the fingers or thumbs. Sometimes the board was hollowed out, forming a resonator, and sometimes a gourd was attached to the instrument and served that purpose. In the specimens exhibited the number of tongues varies from 8 to 19. Some have metal and some have bamboo tongues. All the instruments exhibited are from Africa. No.

167470 is from South Africa and has 14 tongues and 167471 (pl. 13c),
decorated with bits of tin and shell, has 19 tongues. Heli Chatelain
was the collector of 166174 (pl. 13d), from West Africa, and 127190
(pl. 13e) is from the Congo. Brass-headed nails decorate 130946 (pl.
13b), which was a gift from J. H. Camp in 1889. One specimen has a
box instead of a flat board to support the tongues, which are
eight in number, made of bamboo and held in place with strips of
split rattan (166185, pl. 13a). They pass through holes in a stick
which serves as a bridge. It is interesting to compare this primitive instrument with the music box, which consists of a large number
of metal tongues set in vibration by mechanical means. Music boxes
were invented about the beginning of the nineteenth century, probably in Switzerland, the chief place of their production.

A music box may be described as a set of metal tongues cut in a
thin plate of steel commonly called a " comb," and a revolving
cylinder in which are plectra (" pins ") which set the tongues in
vibration. The length of the tongues is carefully graduated, as each
represents a tone, and the position of the plectra on the cylinder
determines which tongue shall be sounded. The cylinder is revolved
either by the continuous turning of a crank or by a spring motor,
commonly designated as clockwork. The first music boxes were
small and not unlike a snuffbox in appearance, and were called
" musical snuffboxes " because they were about the size and shape
of the snuffbox then in use. Small specimens are 55714 (pl. 13f),
which plays two airs, and 55715 (pl. 13h), which plays four airs.
In changing from one air to another a ratchet wheel moves the
cylinder on its axis just far enough for the plectra used in playing
one air to pass between the narrowed ends of the tongues, while
those that play another air are brought into position to strike the
tongues or " teeth of the comb."

This type of instrument pleased the people. The mechanism was
improved and music boxes were made which were capable of playing
six tunes. In the best music boxes the teeth are in groups of 4 to 6,
the teeth of each group being tuned in unison. The pins on the
cylinder strike one after another so rapidly that the ear recognizes
only one sound. This increases the volume of sound and also gives
the effect of a tremolo. Such a specimen is 55717, having 103 teeth
in the comb and capable of playing six tunes. A similar specimen
is 55716 (pl. 13g). The music box and stand (325977) are a bequest
from Mrs. Julian-James, of Washington, D. C. They were made
in Switzerland and the music box plays six tunes.

Section 2. WIND INSTRUMENTS

In this section will be seen a remarkable variety of instruments,
ranging from a primitive whistle to the highly sensitive flute, oboe,

and horn. All these have the same principle of sound production—namely, the vibration of a column of air in a tube. This vibration is produced by blowing with the mouth (rarely with the nose) or by mechanical means, as in the organ. It is interesting and important to note that the column of air is not set in vibration directly by the player's breath or the organ bellows. The vibrations are imparted either by a reed, situated at the point of entry or exit of the air, or through the vibration of bodies which do not form part of the instrument, such as the lips of the player.

WHISTLES

The simplest wind instrument is a primitive whistle, corresponding to the definition of a whistle as " a device in which a current of air is forced through a narrowed aperture or against a thin edge, producing a tone." Whistles are of various shapes, and may or may not have finger holes. The most familiar form of whistle is a straight tube, the instrument being fashioned from a straight stick, a bone, or a section of bamboo, but globular whistles were used by the ancient Aztecs and by other peoples of middle America. It seems possible that such a whistle had its prototype in the globular tree gourd with its hollow shell, which is more abundant than cane in that region. Pottery whistles were frequently modeled in the form of animals, an example of this being 93873 (pl. 14f), in the highly conventionalized form of a reptile. The tail forms the mouthpiece, while above the open end of the tube rises the neck and snakelike head. Another whistle is from Mexico (95721), consisting of a cylindrical tube, the lower end enlarged by a molding. Two pottery wind instruments from ancient Rome are exhibited, 95042 having been taken from an excavation. This whistle is in the shape of a sweet potato, with the mouthpiece projecting from the thickest part. It has twin finger holes and one thumb hole. Uncolored earthenware forms the material of 95154, which is in a long spindle shape with a mouthpiece projecting at its greatest diameter. It has eight finger holes and two thumb holes. Nos. 95331 and 95332 are pottery toy whistles from Spain, in the shape of dogs. A series of modern ocarina are also exhibited, one being illustrated as 95154 (pl. 14j).

A small group of bamboo whistles from Johore, on the Malay Peninsula, was obtained during the World's Columbian Exposition. Several double and triple whistles of bamboo are also exhibited.

It is the custom of the American Indians to make whistles from the wing bone of the eagle or other large birds, and numerous whistles of this type are exhibited. Such a whistle is frequently blown by a medicine man in connection with his treatment of the sick. A whistle has always been an important feature of the ceremonies of the Arapaho and other Plains tribes, and was also used in signaling on the battlefield.

A bone whistle from Costa Rica (15390, pl. 14e) is made of the leg bone of a small mammal, and 4346 (pl. 14a) is made of the thigh bone of a puma and classified as a direct flute.

A remarkable group of wooden whistles without finger holes was brought from the Skidegate and Massetts Indians of the Queen Charlotte Islands by James G. Swan in 1883. These vary in size, but have a general resemblance in shape, 89066, pl. 14g; 89071, pl. 14i; also the double whistle 89070, pl. 14k (Nos. 88873, 88875, 88893, 89060, 89062, 89091, 89226). A carved wooden whistle (89063, pl. 14h) consists of two longitudinal sections and is in the form of a head, the neck reduced to form the mouthpiece. The open mouth forms the sound hole of the whistle. It has one finger hole in the forehead. This whistle was used only at the beginning of the distribution of property at a potlatch. Another carved instrument of this type is 89158 (pl. 14c). The design represents Ooalalla, the mountain demon, the head and chest of the demon being carved on the front and his head and lower limbs on the back of the whistle.

The two small whistles illustrated (233184 and 233185, pl. 14 b and d) are war whistles of the Dahomey, obtained by Dr. Walter Hough at the Louisiana Purchase Exposition. They are made of hardwood, with a decoration of charred lines, chiefly in herringbone pattern.

With the whistles is placed a "bird call" from North Borneo (247773). It is said that "blowing in the mouth tube produces a low mournful sound not unlike the notes of a dove or pigeon. It is used in catching the little green pigeon. The bird, thus decoyed, is noosed by a native." With the whistle are several nooses of vegetable fiber.

FLUTES

PRIMITIVE AND ORIENTAL

The terms "whistle" and "flute" are used with considerable latitude in describing primitive instruments. The following specimens are an interesting group and are classified as "flutes." The thigh bone of a puma is the material forming 4346. The natural cavity of the bone forms the base, and the outside has been worked down. It has three finger holes and is ornamented with a narrow band of incised lines. This is an old specimen, and was brought from British Guiana in 1866 by W. C. McClintock. No. 15825 is also from South America, but probably not so old. It is decorated with beads, feathers, and tassels. A bone flute from ancient Rome (95043) was taken from an excavation. It consists of nine detached sections of bone, one of which is carved with four bearded heads. No. 214486 is made of the leg bones of an animal, but the great antiquity of the specimen makes it uncertain whether this is a complete flute or portions of more than one instrument.

The history of the flute, or pipe, is distinct from that of the whistle. The flute, under different forms and names, has been in use more than 4,000 years. It is interesting to note that wind instruments are never mentioned in connection with the actual worship in the Jewish temple, the three instruments played by the Levites being the cymbals, harp, and lute. The flute or pipe was a favorite instrument among the ancients and is mentioned in the Bible as employed on festival occasions and on those of mourning. "Beaked flutes" were used by the Assyrians and transverse flutes appear in very isolated instances on Egyptian monuments.

The first mention of musical instruments in the Bible occurs in Genesis, iv 21, where the Hebrew word "ugab" is translated organ. Later the same word is translated pipe. That instrument is believed to have been a form of the Pandean pipe, which consists of several reeds of graduated lengths bound together in a horizontal line. The open ends of the reeds were placed side by side and their stopped ends were graduated downward from left to right. The sound was produced by blowing across the open end of the reeds, each of which gave out one tone. The double name of this instrument is due to the ancient Greek tradition ascribing its invention to Pan in connection with a legend of the Arcadian water nymph, Syrinx. The Greek instrument usually consisted of seven pipes, though three to nine were sometimes used. The use of the instrument is widely diffused in both ancient and modern times. Concerning its use in Peru, Charles W. Mead writes: "These pipes are as popular with the modern Indians as they were with their ancestors in the days of the Incas."

Numerous specimens of Pandean pipe (pan pipes) are exhibited, consisting of 3 to 22 reeds, and coming from Java, Japan, Egypt, and the Fiji Archipelago. The specimens illustrated are from Egypt (95187, 95188, pl. 15, h and i)). A particularly interesting specimen from the Fijians is 23940, made of 11 tubes of cane, the longest of which is 15⅞ inches. The pitch of this instrument was taken by Dr. Erich von Hornbostel with his tonometer and found to extend from A (second line below treble staff) to E flat (fourth space treble staff). A pandean pipe from Egypt (95186) consists of 22 tubes of cane ranging from 7¼ to 1¼ inches in length.

The gradual development of the flute may be traced by exhibited specimens. Attention is first directed to 9385, a straight open tube of cane with four finger holes. This specimen came from the Cocopa Indians of Arizona in 1869. From California we have 19756, which is similar except for the decorations. A specimen from the interior of Sumatra (128014) is longer and has four small finger holes and a thumb hole made with a hot iron. In several flutes the upper end is beveled, forming a sharp edge against which the wind is made to impinge. Such specimens are 95727 from Ceylon, which has six finger holes and is ornamented with lines filled with black pigment, and 95696, which has six finger holes arranged in groups of three. The latter is from Damascus. Nos. 95695 and 95150 are also from Syria. An interesting flute of this type is from Morocco (95760). It is decorated with incised lines and patterns, and to it are attached a small bag, a copper coin, and strings of corals. A direct flute from Bulgaria is 95672 (pl. 15e).

The first advance in the making of flutes consisted in cutting a V-shaped notch in the open edge of the top of the pipe, which facilitated the production of sound. This peculiarity is found in ancient Chinese flutes, an excellent example being 54061 (pl. 15a). This is among the valuable articles given to the Museum in 1876 by the Chinese Imperial Centennial Commission. The two holes at the base are for an ornamental cord and tassels. A small flute from Korea has a semicircular notch in the upper edge (95618).

Next in point of development came the idea of partly filling up or plugging the open upper end of the tube and cutting an opening with a sharp edge a little lower down, as in the ordinary whistle. The breath is directed in a thin stream against this lower edge. This principle was known to the Greeks and is seen in ancient Hindu sculptures. The number of finger holes at first was 2, 3, or 4, but the number was afterwards increased to 6 or 8, with a thumb hole at the back. Numerous examples of this type of flute are in the collection.

In order that the air stream might be flat in form when it impinged on the sharp edge of the sound hole, a block was placed inside the flute. This was the "fipple" which characterized a large class of flutes, including the flute à bec, recorder, and flageolet. It will be seen that the block divided the flute into two parts, the air being blown into a cavity from which it issued in a flat stream against the sharp edge or lip of the sound hole.

The American Indians constructed their flutes, both of cane and wood, on this general principle, an example of this being 27844 (pl. 15c), from southern Arizona, described as follows by Mr. Hawley:

A section of cane forming two tubes separated by a joint. Two holes were made from the outside into the cavity with the unbroken septum of the joint between them. A groove is made on the outside from one hole to the other. Covering the upper hole and the groove with a bandage and blowing in the upper tube, the bandage directs the wind from the upper hole against the lower edge of the lower hole, producing a sound like a whistle. The lower tube has three finger holes.

On this specimen the "bandage" is gone, showing the interior structure. The writer has seen flutes of this construction played without the "bandage," the finger of the player being placed over the upper part of the opening. Stiff paper is often tied around the flute to direct the air. Specimens similar to the above are 11314, obtained in 1871 from the Apache, and 107535 from the Mohave. A flute of similar construction is from Burma and has a piece of palm leaf tied over the upper part of the sound hole (95495, pl. 15*f*).

In the typical flute of the American Indians the "bandage" is replaced by a small piece of zinc or other material held in place by a block of wood. A Chippewa flute had a piece of birch bark with a rectangular opening over the sound hole and a bit of silk across the opening, which furnished a sharp, thin lip on which the current of air impinged. Usually the block of wood was secured by a thong or cord passing around the flute, permitting an adjustment by the player; occasionally, however, the block was glued to the flute. The collection contains many examples of this flute, commonly known as the "courting flute" of the Indians. In some instances the block is small and simple, as in 72884 (pl. 15*d*), while in others it is larger and highly ornamented. A large, wooden flute (94005) has a block of this sort carved in the shape of a horse's body and neck and apparently glued to the flute. The lip of the sound hole is a piece of lead bent around the tube, which characterizes this type of Indian flute. An interesting flute (76825) was captured from the Sioux at the battle of White Stone Hill in 1863.

Flutes made of metal are not unknown among the American Indians. No. 96617, obtained from the Apache, is made from the outer half of a gun barrel and 218217, from the Pueblo, is made from a section of gas pipe.

Special attention is directed to the two Moorish flutes in a parchment case (95766-7, pl. 15*g*).

A transverse flute of cane was collected among the Yuma of Arizona and its sound recorded phonographically by the writer. This instrument consists of an open tube of cane with three finger holes. It was held horizontally and blown at the end (325187, pl. 15*b*). Other transverse bamboo flutes have a mouth hole in the side. Such a specimen is 92707 from India. This is the Murali and is said to have been invented by the god Krishna. No. 95210, from Korea, is interesting in that it has a large opening midway between the mouth hole and the first finger hole covered with film or bladder. A metallic cover is bound over this opening with leather thongs. This can be removed, allowing the film to give a reedy quality to the tone of the instrument. Another transverse bamboo flute (4344) is from British Guiana and was collected by W. C. McClintock in 1866.

The collection contains bamboo flutes from Egypt, Korea, China, Ceylon, Syria, Peru, Java, British Guiana, and Sumatra, the East Indies, and the Fiji Archipelago, as well as cane flutes from the Yaqui Indians of Mexico and the Mohave, Pima, Apache, and Cocopa Indians of the United States.

An interesting specimen of a direct bass flute (255713, pl. 16d) from Yokohama, was obtained from Mrs. James M. Flint. It consists of four joints of a section of cane. The lower joint, showing the starting of the roots, is slightly curved and a hole is bored through the solid part into the natural cavity.

A remarkable collection of cane flutes played by the nose was brought from the Fiji Islands about the year 1840 by the Wilkes Exploring Expedition. Several are ornamented with designs in charred lines. The finger holes are 2, 3, 4, 6, 7, and 8 in number. A particularly interesting instrument (23939) is from the Fiji Islands and has two prongs, resembling leaves of corn. Similar specimens are exhibited from Samoa and the Tahiti Society Islands.

VERTICAL FLUTES AND FLAGEOLETS

The European flute of the Middle Ages was the flute à bec, which received its name from the resemblance of the mouthpiece to a bird's beak. It was a fipple flute and had the same general form as the flute of the American Indians. The most familiar example of this flute is the recorder, made in England. The only recorder flute in the collection is 214487, said to have been made in England early in the eighteenth century. It is made of turned cherry in three joints with two bone ferrules. It has seven finger holes and a thumb hole. The bore is conical, largest at the upper end. The tone of recorders is described as " solemn and sweet," and the series comprised four instruments, the discant, alto, tenor, and bass. This form of instrument was superseded by the transverse flute, and its only descendant was the flageolet, which is still common as a toy instrument.

No music of importance has been composed for the flageolet, and it does not appear on orchestral scores.

A true flageolet has four finger holes and two thumb holes. The present collection shows a " D flageolet " of a French model (55637, pl. 16a), and an Italian flageolet (95044) with seven finger holes, collected by Dr. G. Brown Goode. A Javanese flageolet is 95667.

Double flageolets were also used in the nineteenth century. Engel states that " in 1819 Bainbridge took out a patent for the construction of double flageolets." The Museum is fortunate in possessing a double flageolet stamped with the name of " Hastrick," who is said to have been a son-in-law of Bainbridge and who manufactured flageolets in London in 1830–1850. In this instrument (94632, pl. 16b) the tubes are unequal in length, a form of double flageolet which is exceedingly rare. The flageolet consists of a mouth tube and cap of ivory, a head of boxwood, and two parallel tubes inserted in the head. One tube is in one piece 9¾ inches long, the other is in two pieces and is 11⅞ inches long. The shorter tube has six finger holes and five keys, a sixth key being placed in the head above the tube. The longer tube has four finger holes and five keys. The double flageolet with tubes of the same length (237751) is a modern instrument.

TRANSVERSE FLUTES

A transverse flute is shown on the frescoes of the Cathedral of St. Sophia, at Kief, Russia, indicating the use of that instrument in the eleventh century. It did not, however, come into general use until 1636, when the "flute d'allemand," or German flute, became popular. This had a round mouth hole at the side and was held horizontally. It was made of one piece of wood, with a cylindrical base and six finger holes. About the middle of the seventeenth century the base was changed to a conical shape, with its smallest diameter at the foot. The instrument was then made in three parts, or joints, called the head, body, and foot. Extra upper sections could be put in the body, these being of different lengths and correspondingly changing the pitch of the instrument. About 1677 a key was placed in the lower part of the flute, and in 1726 Quantz applied the second key and constructed the head with a sliding joint; he also attached a screw to the cork by which it could be adjusted. The oval mouth hole came into use about 1724.

One of the oldest flutes in the collection is 95297, which was made about 1793 by Grenser, of Dresden, who was the first to make a bass clarinet. This flute has six extra second joints by which the key of the instrument could be changed. The use of the interchangeable second joint was common before the invention of the sliding joint or tuning slide. It is a transverse flute with six finger holes and one thumb hole. No. 219093 is stamped "Georg Waldehauser Straubing 1798." It has six finger holes and one brass key.

To Theobald Boehm the art of flute playing owes "the present system of fingering, the cylinder bore, the silver tube, and much of the beautiful mechanism which have completely revolutionized the instrument and have made the Boehm flute one of the most perfect of musical instruments."[6] The new system of fingering was made known by Boehm in 1832, and the best flutes of the present day are constructed on the Boehm models.

---

[6] Dr. Dayton C. Miller, in translator's introduction to The Flute and Flute Playing, by Theobald Boehm, p. xxv.

Numerous specimens of transverse flutes are exhibited, some made of cocus wood and some of boxwood, while some have the body and foot of "granadillo" wood. A large majority of these were acquired in 1882. Nos. 55629, 55625, and 55628 have a brass sliding joint and screw-adjusted cork; 55627, 55623, and 55630 (pl. 16e) have a sliding joint of German silver, and 55624 (pl. 16c) has no sliding joint. No. 95050 is brass lined and has a cork without a screw to adjust it. A transverse bamboo flute from Pekin (130446, pl. 16f) was collected by Mrs. W. W. Rockhill in 1888.

A "concert flute," an American instrument, is of rosewood, the cork adjusted by a screw. It has 15 lateral openings, 5 of which are closed by the fingers and 10 by silver keys. An interesting old ivory flute in a case (300888), is dated "about 1812," and an example of the rare porcelain flute is 95911.

Four transverse Japanese flutes are exhibited. These are made of bamboo and each has seven finger holes. No. 95809 is lacquered red inside; 93205 (1 and 2) are lacquered black and decorated with designs in raised gold lacquer, and 94,660 is varnished and ornamented with bands of black lacquer. Similar instruments are 93204 (1 and 2, pl. 16g). Nos. 260795 (A and B) are Moro flutes from Mindanao Island and are made of bamboo, the mouth hole and six finger holes made with a burning iron.

The term piccolo (Italian for "little") is commonly applied to the octave flute. The pitch of the piccolo is an octave higher than the pitch of a flute of the same denomination. The two sizes are the C and the E flat piccolo. The piccolo as usually made is a small flute of conical bore with six keys. Piccolos with the Boehm fingering are made both with the conical and the cylindrical bore. Three of these instruments are exhibited. No. 55631 is a C piccolo, and 55632 and 55633 are E-flat piccolos. These are made, respectively, of boxwood and cocus wood.

The fife differs from the piccolo in having a cylindrical base. Strictly speaking, a fife is a small cylinder flute, generally unjointed, with six finger holes and without any keys. It appears to have been introduced into military music early in the sixteenth century by the Swiss, and is said to have been first used by the Swiss troops in the Battle of Marignano in 1515. The true fife, which was generally set in B flat, F, or C, was faulty in intonation, and its place is often taken, in the so-called "flute bands," by small flutes fitted with keys. The flute without keys has continued, however, in military service and in many "fife and drum corps."

A "U. S. Regulation C fife," acquired in 1884, is 93193. It has six finger holes. No. 55746 is also a C fife of the year 1882, and 210179 is a fife stamped "B flat." turned from a single piece of cocus wood slightly tapering from the mouth hole toward the ends which are tipped with German silver ferrules. The bore is cylindrical, and it has six finger holes in line with the mouth hole and arranged in two groups of three.

A "flageolet fife" (55749) is made of brass tubing with a plug of cast lead or pewter.

REED INSTRUMENTS

A large group or family of instruments have, as an important part of their mechanism, a small, thin strip of metal, cane, or wood, which imparts a peculiar quality to the tone. This is called a "reed" and is set in vibration either by the player's breath, as in the clarinet, or by mechanical means, as in the reed organ. The reed is set in the mouth piece of the smaller instruments.

The plant used for reeds, according to Grove's Dictionary, is a tall grass or reed, the Arundo Donax or Sativa, growing in the south of Europe. The chief supply is now obtained from Frejus, on the Mediterranean coast. Other materials have been tried but not found satisfactory in orchestra instruments. Organ reeds were formerly made of hardwood, more recently of brass, German silver, and steel.

The subject of reed instruments is introduced as follows by Mr. Hawley:

Reeds may be divided into two kinds, single and double. There are three kinds of single reeds: (1) The beating reed, as in the clarinet; (2) the free reed, as in the harmonica, accordian, and reed organ; and (3) the ribbon reed, as when a blade of grass is held between the thumbs. The jew's-harp is also a free reed, but is too stiff to be set in vibration by the current of air which passes through the instrument; it is therefore vibrated by the player's hand. There are two kinds of double reeds, the oboe and the bassoon (which differs slightly from it) and the double inverted reed which at present has been found only in Morocco and in the northwest coast of America.

Some of this class of instruments have a reservoir of air to produce a continuous sound, as the bagpipe.

SINGLE REEDS

1. The simplest example of a single beating reed is the reed horn, which has no finger holes. A "reed horn" of the Germans is 214483, made of brass in the form of a cow's horn flattened at the larger end. A brass single beating reed projects from the small end, and is inclosed in a "Pirouette" or cap of German silver screwed on the end of the horn. This kind of horn was used by conductors of railway trains in Germany.

An example of a single beating reed with finger holes is the shepherd's pipe (95045). The body is turned from one piece of wood. It has a conical bore with 8 finger holes, 1 thumb hole, and 3 for ornament in the bell. Its reed is made from cane and it has a bell similar to that of the clarinet. A small instrument of this kind is still used by peasants in the Tyrol. An interesting example of this class is the snake charmer's pipe, used in India (92714, pl. 17*g*). According to Capt. Meadows Taylor, these instruments

are not much used with other musical instruments and belong to snake charmers and various tribes of jugglers, acrobats, and the like. By the snake charmers a few notes only are played, which seem to have the effect of rousing the snakes to action. Usually the cobra de capellos are exhibited and as the reptiles raise themselves on their tails, expand their hoods and wreath themselves to and fro, the player becomes more excited and the motions of the snakes are accelerated by the player's rapidity of execution.

Two pipes of this sort from other countries are 96467 from Russia with a vibrating tongue formed in one side, and 95704 from Cairo, made of a single tube of cane without a reducing joint, and having a conical bell made of tin plate.

The collection contains an interesting group of double pipes with finger holes and a single reed. The two pipes are lashed together and one acts as a drone and has no finger holes, the other is the shorter and has either five or six finger holes. Such an instrument is 94656 from the Arabs in Mesopotamia, while 95702 and 95703 are from Cairo, the former of these being peculiar in that both pipes have finger holes. A Syrian double pipe is 95653, consisting of two pipes of cane lashed side by side. The melody tube is made up of three sections, the lower one is the longest and is pierced with six finger holes, the one next above it is shorter and telescopes into the lower, acting as a reducing joint. The upper joint is the mouth piece, and the single beating reed is formed in its side. The upper part of the other tube is similar but has no finger holes. This tube acts as a drone but has two extension pieces of different lengths. Either can be added or the three may be combined, the various combinations giving the drone three different tones. Other double Syrian pipes made of cane are 95148, 95149, 222167, the first two being about 31 inches long and the third being only about 12 inches in length. A double pipe called the " Bedouins' shepherd pipe " is 93555.

The clarinet is the most familiar instrument of this class, and is the most important instrument of the wind band. It may be described briefly as a cylindrical tube, pierced with many side holes, terminating in a bell and having a single beating reed set in the mouthpiece. The shape of the mouthpiece is that of a conical stopper, flattened on one side to form the table for the reed, and thinned to a chisel edge on the other for convenience to the lips. The table on which the reed lies is not flat but curved backward so as to leave a slit between the end of the mouthpiece and the point of the reed. It is on the vibration of the reed against this curved table that the sound of the instrument depends. The reed itself (a thin, flat strip of the grass already named) is flattened on one side and thinned on the other to a feather edge. The older players secured this to the table with a waxed cord, but the present method is by a double metallic band with two small screws. This use of the beating, single reed was invented late in the seventeenth century by John Christopher Denner, of Nuremberg, Saxony. The Boehm system was adopted to the clarinet by Klose in the early part of the last century.

At present the clarinet family is the most complete among wind instruments in range of compass, color, mobility of tone, and mechanical facilities. The tonal range covers six and one-eighth octaves, and the group comprises seven instruments. The four highest in pitch are straight tubes, and the E-flat alto, the bass, and the contrabass have the tube bent upward and the bell at a slight angle to the tube.[7]

Among the clarinets exhibited are 55620, a C clarinet with 13 keys, and 55621, a B-flat clarinet, 3 inches longer than the C clarinet and, like it, having 6 finger holes, 1 thumb hole, and 13 German silver keys. An alto clarinet in F (95296) from Italy is believed to have been made early in the nineteenth century.

The "Basset horn" (properly called "Corno de Bassetto") was a tenor clarinet standing in F, furnished with additional low keys and a prolonged bore, enabling it to reach the octave C which is equivalent to F below the bass clef. A specimen of this horn is 95295, probably made between 1790 and 1800, obtained in Florence by Dr. G. Brown Goode.

The saxophone is a single-reed instrument made of brass and has a conical tube, its mouthpiece being similar to that of the clarinet. The ophicleide (see p. 49) is supposed to have given the ingenious Sax the idea for the saxophone, as he substituted a reed mouthpiece for the cupped mouthpiece of the ophicleide and made certain other changes, producing the early forms of saxophone about the year 1840. Several of these instruments are exhibited. They resemble the clarinet in mouthpiece but differ from it in fingering. The tone is composite in quality, seeming to unite the tone of reed and brass instruments.

A curious instrument with single reed is the Welsh pibgorn. Specimens of this old instrument are extremely rare, and 214490 (pl. 17a) is a reproduction. It is a tube of wood with a cylindrical bore, having six finger holes and a thumb hole. The lower end of the tube is inserted in a cow's horn for a bell, the open end of which is cut

---

[7] See Arthur A. Clappe, The wind band and its instruments. New York, 1911, pp. 49–59.

to represent the open fanged mouth of a reptile. In the upper end of the tube is inserted a single reed of cane like those used by the Egyptians. On the upper end of the tube is a horn mouthpiece which incloses the reed and prevents the lips from touching it. This was called the "hornpipe" from the horn used at both ends of it, and it was played for a rustic dance which took its name from that of the instrument and was called the hornpipe. An analogous case of the name of a dance being derived from a musical instrument occurs in the word "jig," derived through the French "gigue" from the German "geige" meaning a fiddle.

From the district of Kirvy in Finland we have a hornpipe (95688) which is crudely made, but has a cow's horn for its bell.

2. The second division of single reeds is the free reed which was known in China long before the Christian era. The cheng is one of the oldest Chinese instruments that is still in use and may be regarded as the most ancient species of organ with which we are familiar. According to Chinese tradition it was invented in the reign of the Emperor Hoang-ti, 2700 B. C. This instrument consists of small bamboo reeds projecting above an air chamber shaped like a cup. At one side of this cup is a thick spout and in the base of each bamboo, within the cup or air chamber, is a small free reed. The sound is produced by the player sucking the wind through the spout. Each bamboo has a finger hole at its base, and "speaks" when this is closed and the air drawn forcibly downward through the bamboo and the air chamber. The bamboo tubes vary in height above the body from 5 to 14 inches. An excellent example of the Chinese instrument is 96574 (pl. 17f). The upper ends of the reeds have bone or ivory ferrules and the outer end of the mouthpiece is faced with bone or ivory. It has the usual number of 17 tubes, 4 of which are silent, serving only to strengthen the position of the others. A similar instrument is 94855. A much larger instrument is the "Malay mouth organ" (94931), the cane tubes varying in length above the body from 20 to 35 inches. In the Dyak mouth organ (95903, pl. 17d) the air chamber is a small gourd shell with a slightly curved neck which acts as a mouthpiece. A bundle of six cones are inserted in the upper side of the gourd and the connection is made airtight by packing with wax. The cones rise above the air chamber from 14¾ to 26 inches. The operation of these is similar to the Chinese cheng; the present instrument, however, has a device consisting of a long strip of cane by which the pitch of the tone can be changed. An example of the cheng from Korea (95213) has 16 bamboo tubes, the longest of which is 15 inches in length.

The free reed was first introduced among Europeans at the instance of Professor Kratzebstein, of St. Petersburg, by Kismek, an organ builder of Copenhagen, about the year 1780. Mr. Hawley writes as follows concerning it:

The free reed is invariably made of metal, though it could be made of other material. It consists of a base or reed plate of sheet metal having a somewhat narrow, rectangular opening. Over the opening is fastened a flexible tongue of metal fastened at its base, and of width and length to pass freely through the rectangular opening beneath without touching the sides or end. This tongue is so formed as to lie in its normal position a little above the face of the reed plate. A current of air forced through the opening in the reed causes it to vibrate and the air to escape in puffs or waves, thus producing sound. The pitch of the sound is governed by the formation of the vibrating tongue and not by the length of the column of air. The longer the vibrating tongue the slower will be its vibration and the lower its pitch; the thinner the tongue near its base the slower will be its vibrations; frequently the outer end of the tongue is loaded to produce slower vibrations.

The harmonica, or mouth organ, is a free reed instrument blown by the mouth. It is constructed with rectangular cells arranged in rows. Some instruments have one row of cells and each cell has two reeds, one speaking when the breath is drawn in, the other when the breath is forced out. In other instruments the cells are arranged in two rows, and each cell has one free metallic reed. In one row the reed is inside the cell, and in the other it is outside. Those of one row speak when the breath is forced through them, of the other when it is drawn through them. Harmonicas are made in various sizes, designated as in different keys. The Museum owns a large group of these instruments (not exhibited), which were the gift of J. Howard Foote in 1882. It is said the best harmonicas were made by Richter, of Germany, and several of his manufacture are in this group. Others were made by Langhaumer, of Germany, and Wilhelm Thio, of Vienna. Later these instruments were manufactured by the German Harmonica Company, of New York.

A " concert harmonica " of German make is 55667. This consists of four harmonicas united at right angles to each other. Each harmonica has 12 cells in the outer edge, and brass reed plates. There are two reeds in each cell, one placed inside and the other outside. There is a perforated bone plate in the outer edge of each, and the reed covers are of plain brass. The four wings or harmonicas have each a different key.

The accordion is a free reed instrument operated by means of a keyboard and was invented in 1829 by Damian, of Vienna. Originally it was an extension of the harmonica, in which the reeds were set in vibration by blowing through holes with the mouth. The accordion supplied the air by means of bellows, but the principle of sound production was the same. The essential constructive features of the accordion are a pair of hand bellows, to one side of which is attached a keyboard with keys which vary in number from 5 to 50, operating metal free reeds. Each key controls two notes, one with the inflation and one with the deflation of the bellows. In playing an accordion the right hand is placed over the keyboard while the left hand works the bellows, on the lower side of which are usually to be found two keys which admit wind to other reeds furnishing a simple harmony, usually the chords of the tonic and dominant. Thus the instrument can be played in only one key. An interesting accordion (95040) was obtained in 1892 from Mrs. Mary Mertag, who brought it from Germany in 1850. It has a rectangular body with five rectangular push keys in each end. It has two reeds to each key that differ in pitch and tone, and so arranged with flap valves that when the key is raised the bellows expand and draw the air through only one reed, while compressing the bellows allows the wind to pass through the other reed. It has loop handles of leather on both ends. Other accordions are exhibited, the series being a gift from J. Howard Foote in 1882. One of these (55643) has trumpet-shaped ornaments.

The concertina is a portable instrument of the seraphine family, patented by Sir Charles Wheatstone in 1829. It is hexagonal in shape and has pistons or "touches" on both ends of the bellows. The sound is produced by the pressure of air from the bellows on free metallic reeds. A typical concertina (55645) was a gift from J. Howard Foote and has 10 keys at each end.

An early form of free-reed instrument is the "rocking melodeon," or "elbow melodeon." This instrument was used in America about 1825, and continued until the middle of the century. The exhibited instrument (204639) is stamped with the name of Prescott, who began the manufacture of these instruments in 1836 and continued about 10 years. There seems to have been a distinction between the two forms of melodeon, as we read that "D. Bartlett, who worked for Prescott, later made the elbow melodeon." The air is forced through the reeds by means of bellows which are in two parts, both parts hinged at one end, the parts extending the length of the instrument with their hinges at opposite ends and placed one above the other. The lower part of the bellows is the pump and has a spring; the upper part acts as an air reservoir. The reeds and keyboard are above the bellows, and each key opens a valve that admits the air to its reed. It has 24 natural keys in one row and 17 sharps in the second row; between them is a tablet lettered with the letters of the natural and sharp keys. The range is three octaves and four full notes from 2 F to 2 A.

The invention which contributed most to the placing of music within the reach of everyone was the invention of the melodeon with pedals, and its successor, the cabinet organ. The melodeon was easily played, not requiring any adjustment of tone; it had a large range of tone and its adaptation to all sorts of music and to all occasions gave it a wide appeal. It was an instrument with free reeds, operated by suction, the air being drawn through the pipes, not forced through. The same principle was used in the cabinet organ. The library of the music section contains a catalogue or organs and melodeons published in 1869 by George A. Prince & Co., of Buffalo, N. Y., which announces that 45,000 of these instruments "have been finished and are now in use." The Prince melodeon is designated as a "musical luxury." In the collection is an excellent example of a melodeon with single bellows worked by a pedal (96410) made by C. H. Packard, Campello, North Bridge-. water, Mass.; also a working model of a portion of a reed organ (94649) used by the firm Mason & Hamlin in 1882. This shows the operation of the diapason stop and octave coupler.

A new era in the popularization of music came with the invention of instruments using perforated paper rolls. An early form of this was the clariona or orguinette (72881). This is an automatic free reed instrument whose action is described as follows by Mr. Hawley:

The turning of its crank works a bellows which exhausts the air through the free reeds, at the same time it moves a strip of manila paper over and closes the air channels to the reed. In this strip of paper holes are cut at such points as will admit the wind to the particular reed required to sound the necessary note of the music. The length of the holes in the paper is governed by the duration of the tune desired.

With this is shown a strip of manila paper wound on a spool ready to be placed in the instrument: "This strip has the long and short holes necessary to play 'Home, Sweet Home,' and four other tunes."

The pianola was invented by Edwin S. Votey in 1896, and an instrument was presented to the Museum by the Aeolian Company (324741). Mr. Votey describes the instrument as follows:

The pianola was built for the purpose of playing on the keyboard of any regular piano and operated by means of a perforated music roll through a suitable pneumatic action, actuating a series of finger levers which struck the piano keys the same as a pianist would—the performer supplying the power by the use of foot pedals which enabled him also to vary the force of blow and thereby play loud or soft according to the force applied.

Two other musical instruments using perforated music rolls are the automatic piano (239911) and the "violin virtuosi" (not numbered).

The pipe organ has been called the "king of instruments" and the Museum is fortunate in possessing an instrument of historic as well as musical value (244841). This church organ is said to have been made in England in 1700. It was first used in the old Port Royal Episcopal Church in Virginia and passed from there to Christ Church, Alexandria, where it was in use during George Washington's

time. From there it was taken to the Episcopal Church at Shep-
herdstown, Va., and in the early sixties it was taken by canal to
Hancock, Md., and installed in St. Thomas' Episcopal Church. It
was in use in that church until received by the Museum in 1907 as
a gift from the vestry.

The jew's-harp, as already indicated, is a free reed set in vibration
by the player's hand. It seems probable that the name came from
the French jeu-trompe, implying a toy trumpet. In Scotland, where
it was much used at an early date, it was called a "tromp." This
simple instrument consists of a flexible steel tongue riveted at one
end to a frame of brass or iron. The free end of the tongue is bent
outward at a right angle so as to allow the finger to strike it when
the instrument is placed to the mouth and firmly supported by the
pressure of the frame against the teeth. Mr. Hawley writes that:

> The pitch of the tone is governed by a complicated law of acoustics. The
> vibration of the tongue itself corresponds to a very low sound, but the cavity
> of the mouth is capable of various alterations, causing a series of higher
> reciprocated tones. These are not consecutive diatonic tones, and therefore
> it is necessary to use several instruments of different sizes to produce a
> complete scale. If this is done, it is said that "extremely original and beauti-
> ful effects can be produced."

A group of manufactured jew's-harps of various sizes is exhibited,
as well as jew's-harps of bamboo, the latter showing the use of the
instrument among widely separated peoples.

Among the bamboo jew's-harps are 178242, from Siam. When
played the handle is held in the left hand, resting against the
teeth, and the leaflike spur at the outer end is struck with the
finger of the right hand. Two modern jew's-harps from the island
of Mindanao are 230143 and 232846. In the latter the slip of bamboo
is lashed to a carved wooden openworked handle painted red and
black. A specimen from the State of Johore on the Malay Peninsula is 95707, which is peculiar in that it is a sort of jew's-harp in
which the frame and not the tongue is vibrated. This is accomplished by a string attached to the frame, with a short stick at
the other end. A copy of a bamboo jew's-harp of the island of
Java is 229448, marked "grinding." From the island of Guam we
have 230997, in which the spur struck by the finger is unusually
long. An interesting specimen is 95940, made from a piece of dark
colored bamboo cut to form three prongs, all united at the base.
The inside one is flat, thin, and pointed, and is the tongue. The
outer ends of the other two are lashed together and the tongue
vibrates freely between them. This specimen is from New Guinea.
A particularly old specimen is 19412, obtained in Japan by Gen.
Horace Capron in 1855, and used by the Ainos. The tongue and
frame are of one piece of bamboo, and the tongue is set in vibration by

the jerking of a string of sinew. A similar specimen is 22268, obtained in 1876. Another specimen in which the tongue is vibrated by a string is 23943, from Fiji. The instrument is shaped like a netting shuttle and the tongue is strung with glass beads. A specimen from New Guinea (73428) is shaped like a three-tined fork, the central tine shorter than the outside ones, which are brought together and lashed. The middle tine is thinner at the base to make it more flexible, and apparently was vibrated by a string tied to a hole midway its length. A Moro jew's-harp obtained in 1901 is 208069, with a V-shaped frame that is held against the teeth while the spur is struck with the finger of the right hand to produce the vibration.

It is interesting to note that (except among certain tribes of the northwest coast) the only reed instrument used by the American Indians was the " moose call." Such an instrument obtained among the Chippewa was in the form of a short wooden tube, separable into two sections, with a pointed reed set in the lower section. The reed consisted of a very thin slip of bone or horn, probably that of a deer. It is said that other tribes used a thin strip of birch bark in a similar manner.

3. The single ribbon reed is exemplified by a blade of grass placed between the thumbs and set in vibration by blowing against it. This principle of sound production is said to have been known in ancient times by the Pueblo and other Indian tribes. An instrument obtained from the Indians on Queen Charlotte Islands contains the principle of sound production (20688). Mr. Hawley describes the instrument as follows:

It consists of an oval block of wood divided into five longitudinal sections and lashed together with twine. The sections are so hollowed as to form air passages. The reeds are a strip of narrow silk ribbon passed in and out around the sections and stretched taut across the middle of each air passage. There is a difference in the pitch of the different sections, producing a very discordant sound.

DOUBLE REEDS

The oboe is a wind instrument with a double reed, its form being the result of gradual development from antiquity. Prior to the time of Handel it was the only wind instrument in the orchestra and gave the "tuning A" to the strings, a prerogative which it holds to the present day, although the clarinet has largely displaced it in the family of wood winds. During the Middle Ages the oboe had only three keys. The success of the Boehm system on the flute led Buffet to adopt rings upon the oboe. Numerous improvements followed, until the oboe is now the most delicate and perfect reed instrument that is made. The collection contains an Italian oboe made of boxwood in three joints, with two extra joints, which are, respectively, one-half inch and 1 inch longer than the one in the instrument (95298). It has a conical bore with six finger holes and two brass keys. There are two holes also in the bell. The mouth tube is a tapering brass straight tube inserted in the upper end. An interesting "hautbois or discant Schalmey" from Amsterdam, made in the last half of the eighteenth century, is stamped with the maker's name—E. Terton; above this is a crown and below it the lion of the Netherlands. This specimen is 208185.

The bassoon is the natural bass to the oboe and similar reed instruments. The English and French name (bassoon) is derived from its low pitch, and the Italian and German names (fagotto, fagott) come from its resemblance to a faggot or bundle of sticks. The bassoon consists of five pieces, named, respectively, the crook, wing, butt, long joints, and bell. When fitted together these form a hollow cone about 8 feet long, the internal measurement of a bassoon of the old philharmonic pitch being 93 inches. The bending of the instrument reduced the actual length to a little more than 4 feet. The scale of the instrument is " complicated and capricious," but the musical value of the instrument is very great. One specimen is exhibited (219091), obtained in Italy. Its length is 37¼ inches.

Attention is directed to a " cromorna alto in C " (216389), which has a double reed like a bassoon and seven finger holes. It is covered with leather and the tube is straight except the lower end, which is bent in almost a half circle. This specimen is a reproduction of an Italian instrument made in England during the sixteenth century, and was obtained from Rev. F. W. Galpin, of Hatfield Vicarage, Harlow, England.

Numerous specimens of instruments with double reeds from Asiatic countries are exhibited. None are more interesting than 96655 and 96656, which were presented to the Museum by John B. Henderson. These instruments are part of an entire Chinese orchestra obtained by Mr. Henderson in Pekin. Others of the series are exhibited in other sections.

A double reed of palm leaf characterizes 54055, and the outside of the tube is ornamented with metal spheres. The Chinese hautbois (95827, pl. 17b) is of rosewood and the double reed is made from a stalk of grass. An extra double reed is with this instrument. Another Chinese oboe is 54058, a gift of the Chinese Imperial Centennial Committee in 1876. Siamese instruments of this class are 4001, 54067, and 54068, and a Korean hautbois is 95212, its mouthpiece a tapering brass tube with a double reed made of a stalk of grass or cereal. A circular flat disk of metal on the mouth tube forms the guard plate. The bell is of brass and is loose on the tube. Two Malay hautbois are 95934 and 94935, the former having its double reed made from a stalk of grass or cereal. Another Malay hautbois (94932) has the double reed made of two pieces of palm leaf fastened on the small end of the mouth tube. From Burma is shown a hautbois with double reed of palm leaf (95489), and a Singhalese instrument is 95713. A Turkish hautbois is 95136 with double reed of grass stalk. A Moorish instrument is 95763, and an oboe from Egypt is 95196.

In this, as in other classes of musical instruments, there is an interesting Russian group from the Georgians, living at Tiflis in the Caucasus. These are 94767, 94768, and 72979. The latter is a cylindrical tube of wood, its lower end terminating in a ball, within which the tube expands. The mouthpiece of a similar instrument (72978) is

made from a stalk of Dourrahma species of maize. The lower end is cut just below a joint; above the joint it is constructed by the tight winding of a cord. When the stalk was green, about an inch above this, the cuticle was removed. The upper part is pressed flat, thus forming a double reed. A disk of pearl has a hole made in its center to fit the flattened portion of the mouthpiece. This is forced on the upper end and forms a guide for the length to be inserted in the mouth. A keeper formed of a short section of reed is split and hollowed to fit the end of the reed, then it is slashed together at each end with a small cord or thread.

Two Italian double-reed instruments, not classified as oboe, are 95300 and 95301, made of unvarnished wood, in two or three pieces, and having four finger holes.

The double-reed instruments of primitive type are chiefly from the Skidegate and Massetts Indians of the Queen Charlotte Islands and the Bellabella Indians of British Columbia, the specimens having been collected by James G. Swan in 1875 and 1883–84. These instruments are made of two longitudinal sections of wood, each section forming half of a flattened tube and also one of the sides or valves of a double reed. The two strips of wood are lashed together with split spruce roots. One instrument (20689) is shaped somewhat like a paddle; the halves are excavated to form two air passages starting from the lower end and ending in one air passage before the top is reached. The double-reed instruments 88876 and 88878 are used in masquerades and other ceremonies. A large instrument (88894) is made of two strips of wood lashed together with split spruce roots, and afterwards the tube portion is covered with a coarse tow-like fiber loosely wound around it. The bell-like form of 20695 suggests that it is copied from some European instrument.

A curious example is 89064, consisting of a short tube of wood with double reeds fitted inside it. This tube is inserted in place of the nozzle on a pair of common hand bellows. The boards of the bellows are painted with the conventionalized bear.

Several instruments in this group have inverted double reeds, these being 20690, 89057, and 89059.

WIND REVOLVING REED

A peculiar type of instrument is the " wind revolving reed," the principal example being the " bull-roarer " or " whizzer " of the North American Indians, which consisted of a wooden blade attached to a long cord. This cord may be held in the hand as the blade is swung in the air, but it is usually attached to a handle. Simple as this contrivance may appear, it has a deep significance in many Indian tribes. It is a sacred implement, associated with the winds and the thunder. To the Navaho its whizzing sound represents the voice of the thunderbird, while to the Hopi it represents the wind that accompanies a thunderstorm. At a Papago ceremony in petition for rain the bull-roarers gave the signals for the people to assemble. Sixty or more of them were used at a time, and the sound as they swung through the air was said to be like " the sounds in the clouds " before the coming of rain. The specimens exhibited are considerably smaller than those used in this ceremony. No. 325401 is from the Yuma and has the blade stained dark like a storm cloud and notched like the lightning. This blade is attached by a long cord to a stick which was held in the hand. From the Ute Indians we have 10773, collected by Maj. J. W. Powell.

From the Apache we have two blades (215672) attached to cords, suggesting that they were swung from the hand instead of a stick. One blade has the top cut in the outline of a human head, the mouth being perforated for the cord. On the reverse of the other blade are long, wavy lines, said to represent lightning and also the hair of the wind god. The blade with the cord is also used by the Makah, living on Cape Flattery.

BAGPIPE

The bagpipe occupies a peculiar place among musical instruments, as it contains tubes with fixed tones, tubes on which a melody can be played, and a windbag which holds the air and delivers it to these tubes. The windbag is inflated either by the player's breath or by a small pair of bellows placed beneath one arm, while the windbag is under the other arm. In this form the instrument contains all the essentials of an organ. This principle of tone production has come down from antiquity. Nero is said to have played on it, and the bagpipe appears on a coin of his time.

Although the bagpipe is widely distributed, it has been from early times the special instrument of the Celtic races. It appears to have been in use in Ireland in the year 1300, and a Celtic pipe of the fifteenth century is still in existence, but the instrument is most familiarly associated with Scotland. Many times have the bagpipes led the Scottish troops to victory. It is said that "the last funeral at which a piper officiated in the highlands of Perthshire was that of the famous Rob Roy, who died in 1736." The highest form of bagpipe music is the pibroch, a series of variations founded on a theme called the "urlas" and very difficult to play properly.

The highland bagpipe, which is a typical instrument, consists of a valved tube leading from the mouth to a leather air-tight bag which has five orifices into which are bound five short tubes or "stocks." Into these five stocks are fitted the blowpipe, three long drones, and the melody pipe, which is also called the "chaunter." The player inflates the windbag through the blowpipe, which is the only pipe not fitted with a reed. The three drones have single reeds and the chaunter has a double reed. Each drone is tuned by a slider on the pipe, and they usually give the keynote and its fifth and octave. They, of course, sound continuously while the melody is being played on the chaunter, and are of lengths corresponding to their pitch, the longest being about 3 feet. When the instrument is played these project above the shoulder of the player and diverge from each other like a fan. The chaunter is a conical wooden tube about 14 inches long, pierced with 8 sounding holes, 7 in front for the fingers and 1 at the top, behind, for the thumb of the right hand. The compass is only 9 tones, from G (second line treble staff) to A above the treble staff. It is said that the tones do not form a "scale," but represent (as nearly as can be described) the major chords of G and A with an extra tone "in the neighborhood of F or F sharp."

The Northumbrian or border pipe is a far more accurate instrument than the highland pipe, but all bagpipe music is distinctive and any attempt to adapt it to a musical system is unfortunate. "There is good ground to believe that any attempt to accommodate the bagpipe to modern scale notation would only result in a total loss of its archaic, semibarbarous, and stimulating character." Until recently the music for the bagpipe was taught by a language of its own, each note having a name, such as "hodroho," "hanin," "hiechin," "hachin," etc. The Irish bagpipe (according to Glen) was entirely different from the Scotch.

The Museum owns a remarkable group of six bagpipes, being one each of the Scotch, French, Italian, Tunisian, Syrian, and modern Greek, four of which are exhibited in this section.

A "Great highland bagpipe" (94891, pl. 17c) was probably made about 1745. The bag is of leather, covered with green plaid cloth. The French instrument (204152) has a bag of tanned leather covered with an outer case of maroon velvet trimmed with yellow silk braid and fringe. The tubes are inserted in an oval stock, and all are inlaid with designs in tin or pewter.

The Tunisian bagpipe (95141) is a valuable instrument, deposited by Dr. Cyrus Adler in 1891. The bag is the tanned skin of a kid removed entire from the front of the hind quarters to the neck. The mouth tube is of brass, but the others are of cane, all being inserted into a block of wood forced into the neck opening of the hide. It has two chaunters, each with five holes, and at the end of each chaunter is fitted the tip of a horn, like a flaring bell.

From the Syrians we have 95697 (pl. 17e), which was exhibited in the " Streets of Cairo " at the World's Columbian Exposition at Chicago in 1893. The bag is the skin of a small animal with the hair side out. The mouth tube is of turned wood and the other tubes are of cane, having a single beating reed formed in the side of the cane. Each tube has a bell formed from the tip of a horn.

The manner of playing the bagpipe is illustrated by a figure of an Italian peasant (pl. 18).

HAND ORGAN

The hand organ is supposed to date from the beginning of the eighteenth century. Its mechanism resembles that of a music box in having a cylinder armed on its outside with pins or staples and placed horizontally. It differs from the music box in the substitution of reeds and pipes for the " comb " with its metal tongues of various lengths, also in having a wind chest with bellows. A hand organ is played by turning a crank, which operates both the cylinders and the bellows. The wooden cylinder revolves slowly, and in so doing the pins or staples raise certain trigger-shaped keys which open valves that allow the wind from the wind chest to enter the desired pipes. The cylinder and its shaft can be moved endwise, bringing the pins into position for the playing of several tunes.

A particularly interesting example of this instrument is 284788, which was made by Job Frienlel, of Vienna, given to Theodorus Bailey Myers in 1850, and presented to the Museum by Mrs. Julian-James. It has a single pressure bellows. The reed chamber is in the fixed part of the wind chest, and the free reeds are fastened to the upper board or cover of the wind chest, a small hole being made in the cover directly under each reed. These holes are closed by valves which are operated by the pegs on the wooden cylinder.

Three hand organs from Florence, Italy, are exhibited and were collected by Dr. G. Brown Goode of the United States National Museum. These instruments have double-acting bellows and flue and reed pipes. The flue pipes have a whistle head and are of two kinds, the open at the outer end and the closed. The reed pipes have a single beating reed in the foot. The little automatons on 95302 are moved by clockwork. This instrument has only flue pipes. The larger instruments, 95303 (pl. 47*b*) and 95304, which is considerably larger, have a rectangular base which contains the cylinder, bellows, and air chest, while the upright part contains the pipes. These instruments have both flue and reed pipes, and are constructed to play seven and nine tunes, respectively.

HORNS

The subject of horns is introduced as follows by Mr. Hawley:

Horns of civilized nations generally have a cupped mouthpiece consisting of a small conical or conoidal cup with a small opening in its bottom, the apex of the cone. Some have a small or hemispherical or shallow concave cup. This mouthpiece is sometimes made in the material of the horn, but more often it is separable and inserted in the upper end of the tube. In horns of some savage nations such a mouthpiece is lacking, and the opening into the bore of the tube is large enough to receive a greater portion of the lips.

PRIMITIVE HORNS

A simple horn is one in which the length of the column of air is always the same. Such a horn produces only the fundamental tone and its harmonics. The longer the column of air (to a certain extent) the lower will be the fundamental tone of the horn and the greater the number of harmonics. The oldest example of a simple horn is the Hebrew shofar (154402, pl. 19*a*). This is made of a ram's horn, blown through the small end, and has a cupped mouthpiece. The natural cavity of the horn forms the bore and the outside has been worked down thin so that it conforms to the shape of the cavity. According to Dr. I. M. Casanowicz " the most ancient and frequent use of the shofar was for military purposes, to give the signal for the rallying of the people and for attacking and pursuing the enemy." [8] The shofar was also used for the announcement of Jewish feasts and, with other musical instruments, it accompanied the song of praise in the temple. The first mention of the shofar is in Exodus xix, 16, and the word is frequently and erroneously translated " trumpet " or " cornet." In this and the three horns next following, a cupped mouthpiece is formed by enlarging the natural cavity of the horn. No. 95694 (pl. 19*b*) is a Dervish horn from Damascus, with the lower end cut like a swallow's tail. A Dervish horn from Egypt is shown in 95198 (pl. 19*e*). The flattened horn is probably that of the African goat. A slightly different horn is 92709 from Calcutta. This is a rather short black horn from an ox or buffalo. The tip has been cut off at the commencement of the

---

[8] Annual Report, Smithsonian Institute, 1922, p. 487.

cavity and a cupped mouthpiece formed with a hot iron. Tagore says this was the favorite instrument of the god Shiva.

Another type of simple horn made from the tusks or horns of animals is blown through a mouth hole on the inside of the curve of the natural horn. Notable among these are horns made from elephant's tusks, which were used as war and signal horns. The natural cavity forms the bore of the horn and a mouth hole is cut in the concave side, not far from the tip of the horn. In some specimens a small hole has been made from the tip of the horn to the natural cavity. It is said that the pitch of the horn is affected by closing this opening with the thumb. The exterior surface of the horn is worked down to conform to the lines of the cavity except around the mouth hole, where a thick ridge is left. The mouth hole is somewhat elliptical in shape and this ridge, in some instances, resembles a pair of thick lips.

The largest horn of elephant ivory is 127195 (pl. 19g), which is 44 inches long and about 4 inches in diameter at the opening. The splendid sweep of the curve suggests the size of the elephant that once carried the tusk. This specimen was obtained in 1885 and came from Stanley Falls, on the Congo River, in Africa. No. 127192 is a small horn from the same locality. This has a small hole extending from the tip into the cavity and is decorated with a carved band around the opening. Next to the longest horn in the group is 174795 (pl. 19c) from the Lukenia River, in Congo, Africa. This is more than 35 inches long and would have a powerful tone: The tip is fashioned like a spearhead. Four similar horns were obtained from this locality and show slight variations in size and outline (174791, 174792, 174793, 174795). These are particularly beautiful in coloring, with the mellow tints that are seen only in old ivory.

Two specimens from the French Congo are slightly different in workmanship. No. 95231 (pl. 19f) is octagonal in a portion of its outer surface, and 95232 is carved on the tip with a human face. No. 5412 is of medium size, but is very dark ivory and a particularly handsome specimen. It is ornamented with incised lines and suspended by a cord made of human hair. With these are shown four horns from Africa which have rectangular mouth holes on the inside of the curves. No. 4960 has the outside of the horn in its natural condition. Nos. 95228, 95229, and 95230 "are used by travelers, especially by common people traveling in canoes."

Another form of simple horn is the " conch shell trumpet," widely distributed and associated with war and religious ceremonies. The natural cavity of the shell forms the base and the mouth hole is usually at the apex, though three of the specimens exhibited have a mouth hole at the same side as the opening of the shell. More than five varieties of shell may be seen in the collection, which comprises specimens from the Fiji Archipelago, Korea, Burma, India, the Samoan Islands, and the Indo-Pacific. The largest number are made from the Triton shell (*Triton tritonis* Linnaeus). Three specimens obtained about 1840 have the mouth hole in the side of the shell, all the other specimens have the apex broken or cut off, thus forming a cupped mouthpiece. These are 3466 (*Triton variegatum*), (pl. 19*h*) a particularly handsome shell from the Samoan Islands; 2906 (*Triton tritonis*), about the same size, from the Fiji Archipelago; and 2908, smaller and from the same locality, said to have been used to rally warriors in battle. The three having a mouth hole formed by grinding off the apex of the shell are 95621, from Korea, covered with a network of red cord; 23904, which is Fijian, and 95152, from the Indo-Pacific.

It is said that 92713, from Calcutta, was used in religious ceremonies. The shell is *Pterocera* Lamarck, No. 95509 has the top or cone of the shell bronzed. The shell is *Turbinella pyram* and it is from Rangoon, in British Burma.

No. 92712 (pl. 19*d*) is an ancient Hindu war horn from India. It is made from the "helmet shell" (*Casis* Lamarck), which is thought by the Hindus to resemble the mouth of a cow, and is so named. Cameos are frequently cut from this sort of shell.

SIMPLE HORNS

A trumpet is shown on the Arch of Titus, and this sculpture is believed to be the oldest representation of such a musical instrument. It is a long, slender tube, slightly flaring, with a cupped mouthpiece. Doctor Casanowicz states "the trumpet was the first instrument expressly ordered in the Pentateuch (Numbers x, 1–10). . . . It was almost exclusively a priestly instrument. Its primary use was for giving signals for the people to assemble, but was appropriated to religious services." The form of the ancient Hebrew trumpet was continued in the Roman tuba and in the clarion of the Middle Ages. A specimen of clarion (95294, pl. 20*a*) was collected in Florence by Dr. G. Brown Goode, and in the catalogue is dated 1411. It is 52¾ inches long. The shape of the instrument was well adapted to the carrying of a banner, and in the age of chivalry it was customary for heralds to precede the nobility blowing clarions with banners which displayed the arms or heraldic device of the nobleman.

A particularly interesting form of simple horn is the long slender Alpine horn, used by the mountaineers for signaling and for assembling their herds. The tones of the instrument can be heard a long distance and are made more picturesque by the echoes of the mountains. The melodies played on these horns are called "Songs of the Swiss herdsmen." Two specimens are exhibited, both being made by Hug Bros., of St. Gallen, Switzerland. The older type is a straight conical tube, 96¼ inches long, with the bell turned at a right angle (95512). It is made of thin fir, the outside wound with a ribbon or splint of thin hardwood, and has a cupped mouthpiece made of turned hardwood which is separable from the horn. A second Alpine horn, believed to be of modern form, has the tube bent on itself, making a horn only about 37 inches long (95513, pl. 20b). This is less difficult to handle and is used chiefly in Uri, Schwyz, and Unterwalden. With the Alpine horns is shown a Dutch horn which is about 39 inches long and has no separable mouthpiece (95812). It is a tapering tube built up of five thin flat and tapering staves of wood hooped by bands of withes. The surface is painted brown and decorated in colors. This horn was used by the Hollanders in their Christmas ceremonies.

The folding of the tube, which revolutionized the development of the whole family of brass instruments was known to the Romans in the first century of our era, but, according to Galpin, "it seems almost certain that, like some of the arts of classic times, it was put aside and forgotten when the great empire fell. Just before or after the year 1300, however, the folded form appears again in northern Italy, where a great revival of art and industry had begun." The rediscovery of the form is attributed to an oriental source.

Two metal horns with folded tubes are illustrated. The smaller (55605, pl. 20d) is a C Infantry bugle, "U. S. Army Regulation style, 1860," and the larger (96492 pl. 20f) is a trumpet from Thibet made of eight sections of brass with lapped and soldered joints, the edge of the bell ornamented with leaf points in repoussée. An Italian bugle is 95271.

HORNS WITH SLIDE, FINGER HOLES, KEYS, AND VALVES

On a simple tube, as described in the preceding paragraphs, it is impossible to produce the diatonic scale except in the highest harmonics which are extremely fatiguing to play and faulty in their intonation. Hence mechanical means were devised for lengthening or shortening the tube, whereby a lower or higher series of natural harmonics could be obtained and the gaps in the range of the instrument filled up. The earliest attempt in this direction and a system retained to our own day was the formation of a slide in one part of the tube, which could be extended and drawn in at pleasure. Some writers have traced this first improvement to the Spartan bard, Tyrtaeus, who lived 700 B. C., and it appears that the Romans knew of it. In the Middle Ages such an instrument was called a sackbut, later the instrument was improved and the term "trombone " came into use. The sackbut (or trombone) was evolved from the trumpet the year 1300.

The collection contains a "B flat tenor trombone with slide " (55603, pl. 21h), in which the slides have seven different positions; and a "slide trumpet B natural, high pitch," acquired in 1905 (237756). The slide is drawn in by two coiled springs placed in a closed brass box between the body and the coil. According to Walter Smith, of the United States Marine Band, the slide lowers the natural tone of this instrument a whole tone in pitch.

In Europe during the seventeenth century another means of obtaining a complete scale came into favor. Holes were pierced in the side of a tube and covered with the fingers as in the flute, changing the length of the column of air. The instruments constructed on this principle were called cornets (cornetto) and were of various lengths and shapes, so as to form a complete choir among themselves. Galpin states that "the tone of the cornetto in the hands of an experienced player was much admired; 'it resembles the brightness of a sunbeam piercing the darkness when one hears it among the voices in the cathedral, churches, and chapels.'" In the accounts of Westminster Abbey for the year 1664 there is the entry, "Paied to John Hill for playing on ye Cornett in ye churche this year P. 4." [9]

The simplest form of the instrument was the "tenor cornet" (233535), a straight conical tube of wood covered with leather, and having six finger holes and a thumb hole. A larger instrument of this type was called the Corno Torti or Cornet à Bouquin, and was used in the seventeenth century. Examples of this horn are 233549 and 233550, the former covered with leather and the latter painted. black. The instrument usually had six holes for the fingers and one thumb hole.

The deep bass member of this series of instruments continued in use until a much later date than the cornetto. Under the name of "serpent" it assisted the village choirs. According to Mersenne, a seventeenth century writer, "the sound of it is strong enough to drown 20 robust voices, being animated by the breath of a boy, and yet may be tempered to the softness of the sweetest voice." Like the old cornetto, it was constructed of wood covered with skin or leather. The serpent (54252, pl. 21e), is a very crooked wooden leather-covered tube with a conical base with six finger holes and three keys. It has an ivory cup-shaped mouthpiece fitted to a cylindrical brass tube which can be moved in or out to adjust the pitch. The tube is curved to bring the finger holes within reach, as well as to make the instrument more compact. The principle of the "serpent" was transferred in 1780 to an instrument made of wood in

---

[9] Crystal Palace Handbook for 1900, p. 92.

the shape of a bassoon, and in 1880 a very similar instrument, but in metal, was introduced in England and called the English bass horn. In 1817 additional keys were added to the bass horn, its bore was enlarged, its length increased, and the resultant instrument was the ophicleide, the last of this interesting group of instruments which has been abandoned for many years. An ophicleide is exhibited (292226) which has a tubing length of 109¾ inches. All its lateral openings are opened or closed by finger keys. This instrument was the property of George Warren, who bought it for $35 in 1842, and played it in the Unitarian Church and the town band of Weston, Middlesex County, Mass., until about the year 1850. It was presented to the Museum by his daughters in 1916.

The keyed bugle represented another endeavor to increase the number of tones obtainable in a horn. When Joseph Halliday, the bandmaster of the Cavan Militia in England, was experimenting with an old field trumpet he discovered accidentally that by making holes in the horn he could produce additional tones. This took place in 1810. Later he patented an invention by which keys controlling the side holes were added to the bugle, so that the chromatic degrees between the second and third harmonics could be obtained. This instrument was called the keyed bugle, and became the leading instrument in the military and town bands of England as well as the popular accompaniment of the old stage coach. Thus the trumpet, which is the traditional instrument of the cavalry, and the bugle, which is the corresponding instrument of the infantry, became keyed instruments.

Two instruments listed as "Key bugle in E flat" are 95580, said to belong to the period 1828–1840, and 237755, which was obtained in 1905. An instrument made of tortoise shell with nine brass keys (251395) was transferred from the Patent Office in 1908.

We will now trace the development of another type of horn, a development which took place during the same period as that of the keyed trumpet and bugle. The French, during the seventeenth century, carefully studied the horn for use in the chase. Early in the eighteenth century it was recognized as a true instrument of music and found its place in the orchestra. The difficulty to be overcome was, of course, the imperfect character of its natural scale. Various lengths of tubing were added by which it could be set in any desired key, but even then the scale could only be perfected by the insertion of the hand into the bell, thereby raising the natural tone a half tone or a whole tone, as desired. This device was first suggested by Hampl, of Dresden, about 1770, who discovered it when attempting to produce a softer tone by putting a pad of cotton wool into the bell. The tones thus produced were called "hand notes," and in

France they were called "muffled sounds" because of their peculiar quality. Composers wrote the horn parts so that when weird or mysterious effects were required they employed "hand notes," while in a frank and joyous mood they used the "open sounds." An Italian hunter's horn is 95270, which has a sliding joint to adjust the pitch and free the horn from water. A "French horn" obtained in Italy, and of the type popularly associated with the chase, is 95319 (pl. 20e) with bell painted red on the inside. A small French horn is exhibited. The French horn as a concert instrument is unique for compass and beautiful velvety quality of tone. It is employed in a quartet of first, second, third, and fourth horns where a composer desires smooth, sustained harmonics and particularly beautiful blending of tone.

As said by Galpin, " all these principles and devices, whether slide, holes, keys, or hand, have had to give way, more or less, to the great invention of the nineteenth century—the valve principle. The valves act as little taps which, when moved by a lever or piston, direct the wind into additional lengths of tubing and allow it to return into the instrument and out at the bell." Invented about 1815 by a Silesian, Blumel, improved by the German horn player, Stolzel, and an English farmer, John Shaw, it was perfected by the Belgian family Sax, who have given their name to the Sax horns and other wind instruments, including the modern Saxophones. Stanley writes that at first only two valves were used, in 1829 the number was incerased to three and in 1835 to five valves. The rotary (swivel) valve was invented in 1832 by Johana Riedt, of Vienna, had a brief popularity, and gave way to a return of the former valve, though it was still used in 1900 by German and Austrian bands. By the employment of one or the other of these devices, in combination with tubes of various size in length and bore, a great variety of military instruments and one or two important, orchestral instruments of the tuba class have been produced. An E-flat alto saxophone received in 1901 is 210928 (pl. 21d), and a B-flat tenor saxophone of the same year is 210929 (pl. 21f). A soprano saxophone with straight tube is 210927.

Two interesting Italian horns with valves are shown. No. 95276 is dated " since 1827 " and has rotary valves. The horn is held upright when played. A metal bar connects the finger key to the rotating cylinder. This kind of valve is called Durch ventil by the Germans and Cylindre a rotation by the French. No. 95273, dated " about 1837," has three double-piston valves which lower the tone respectively a tone, a half tone, and a tone and a half. Other combinations lower the tone still greater degrees. This system of double tubular piston valves is called in Germany " Weiner ventil," and was much admired in Belgium.

The application of valves to the old post horn has given us the cornopean, or cornet à piston. The post horn, its tube bent in two rounds, is shown as 72877. A cornopean in E flat with two valves is 54255 (pl. 21g). Its piston valves are of the kind called "schubventil," which were invented by Henri Stolzel, of Germany, in 1825. In this kind of valve the wind may enter at the bottom of the first valve and leave at the bottom of the second valve. The first valve lowers the pitch a semitone and the second valve lowers it a whole tone. No. 55608 is a Challenge B-flat cornet, and 237757 is a B-flat cornet with double piston valves. Each valve has two cylinders and two tubular pistons of the kind called weiner ventil. The scale of instruments with but two valves had certain gaps, which were filled later by additional valves. A B-flat tenor trombone with three piston valves is 55604, these valves being the sort invented in 1833.

An American cornet (E flat) of the military style in use from 1850 to 1870 is 72875. It has three rotary valves with a top action. An E-flat cornet acquired in 1882 and labeled "Style since 1860," is 55596 (pl. 21a), having three rotary valves. A B-flat cornet of the same period is 55595 (pl. 21b). These are brass, nickel plated. A Challenge E-flat cornet acquired in 1882 has three piston valves of the style invented by F. Besson, of Paris, about the year 1850 and improved in 1854.

The cornet à piston is said to be a "hybrid between the high-pitched trumpet and the bugle." It is a facile instrument and double tongueing is one of its popular means of display. It has a harmonic compass from middle C to C above the treble clef and can go higher, but with difficulty.

A valved trumpet marked "alto B flat" is 214566. It has three rotary valves. The valve cylinders, action, and part of the tubing are silver plated and the cylinder heads and finger plates are inlaid with pearl. The collection contains four E-flat alto horns. No. 55587 is the American military style from 1850 to 1870, with bell carried over the shoulder. It is made of brass, nickel plated, and has three rotary valves. No. 55598 is marked "American style since 1875," and was played with the bell upright. It was acquired in 1882. An E-flat alto horn (55597, pl. 21c) is "American style since 1860." No. 55609 is a Challenge light piston E-flat alto horn, tubing length 77¾ inches. It has three light piston valves.

A Challenge light piston B-flat tenor trombone is 55614, made of brass, silver plated, with portions gold plated. It has three piston valves of the style invented by F. Besson about 1850, already noted.

Two B-flat baritone horns are exhibited. No. 55589 is the American military band style with the bell over the shoulder, used from 1850 to 1870. It is made of German silver with three rotary valves.

No. 55600 is "American style since 1875." When played the bell is held upright.

In the horns will be found a "Challenge light piston B-flat euphonium, Courtois model," made of brass, silver plated, with mouthpiece, finger buttons, and water key gold plated (55612). The bell is held upright. It differs from the "baritone" in having a larger base but has the same pitch.

As a contra bass, or double bass horn, we have 55613, which is similar in form and construction to 55612, but much lower in pitch. The bell was held upright. It is called a bombardon. An "E-flat contra bass or bombardon" is 55590, which is 53 inches in length. It is the American military band style from 1850 to 1870 and was played with the bell over the shoulder. A B-flat contra bass helicon is 55592, made of German silver, in Germany. The tube is formed in a coil 34 inches in diameter, sufficiently large to encircle the player, the coil resting on his left shoulder and passing under his right arm with the bell upright. It has three rotary valves and a conical base from the valves to the bell. The valves have the cycle action.

A brass horn from Barcelona, Spain (261730), has a windway of about $89\frac{5}{16}$ inches and a bell diameter of $7\frac{3}{8}$ inches. It has 3 rotary valves and was played with the bell toward the front.

An interesting group of oriental horns is exhibited. The horn is not one of the ancient instruments of China, but the collection contains two Chinese horns which are different from those obtained in any other country. No. 54053 is a tube of sheet brass in two joints soldered together with a crook, the lower end expanding into a bell. The mouthpiece is a flat disk 2 inches in diameter with a hemispherical cup in its center. It is said that a Chinese player took all the disk in his mouth, the cup resting against his gums. No. 54053 is a Chinese trombone differing from the preceding in being straight instead of curved. A Siamese trumpet is shown as 27293 (pl. 20c), a gift from the King of Siam. A Korean trombone is 95209, a straight conical tube in two sections, the upper section sliding into or "telescoping" the lower section. The cupped mouthpiece is like that of the Chinese horns. The specimen was collected by Col. Augustine Heard, United States Legation, Seoul, Korea, in 1891. A Burmese trumpet is 95507, a conical tube in five sections, painted in different colors. It has three rude finger holes in the first section. From Bengal, India, is 92710, a horn made of very thin copper in five curved sections which are jointed together, forming two sections which can be adjusted to form a circle or serpentine figure. It has no bell and there are pairs of triangular rings at the large end and at each joint. These rings are hollow and inclose loose pebbles. The outside is painted with flowers, etc., in colors on a brown ground.

It is used universally throughout India in religious processions, both by the Mohammedans and Hindus; it is also blown by watchmen at sunset and at certain hours of the night. Wailing blasts from this horn are sounded at the cremations of Hindu princes and at the funerals of the lower classes or castes. The tone is not unlike an ordinary bugle, but has more power and compass. A native horn of the Sumatrans is 96452, consisting of three conical tubes sliding one within the other. The bell is flaring and the instrument so curved that when it is played the bell faces the player. The tube is ornamented with hollow rings. According to North China Branch Royal Asiatic Society (p. 100), "the sliding tubes of these instruments are not meant to change their notes but to reduce their lengths when not in use."

The Filipinos in recent times have made a horn out of bamboo and placed outside it two pieces of rattan bent in ovals, imitating the coils of a military horn, also three short pieces of bamboo in imitation of piston valves. No wind passes through these false coils and valves. One end of the bamboo is removed and the "horn" is blown through a short piece of bamboo inserted in its side. These horns vary in size. No. 95052 is a "bass horn" and 95057 an "alto horn," the latter differing in size and also in being split into eight sections a third of its length. This produces a reedy tone in the instrument.

SECTION 3. DRUMS AND OTHER VIBRATING MEMBRANES

No musical instrument has preserved its identity from ancient times so clearly as the drum. It is commonly regarded as a martial instrument, but from early times has been associated with the religion and ceremonies of many peoples. Under the name of tabret or timbrel it is mentioned frequently in the Old Testament, but, according to Dr. I. M. Casanowicz, it "appears to have had no place in the religious services of the tabernacle or the temple." It was "used chiefly by women, especially in dances and public processions." The timbrel shown on Egyptian monuments is four sided as well as circular in shape. The sculpture and literature of Egypt, Assyria, Greece, and Rome indicate the early use of the drum in those countries, but it was not introduced into Europe until a comparatively modern time. Perhaps the largest variety of drums comes from China and Siam, where the drum is connected with religion and is also used in connection with theatrical performances. It was used in the time of Confucius, and is said to have been introduced into Japan from China. Viewing the history and development of the drum in its entirety we note that the general tendency has been to shorten the length of the drum shell and to increase the diameter of the head.

Drums are of three distinct types: Kettledrums, having a head of hide or other substance stretched across the opening of a hemispherical vessel; drums with one head, having a head stretched across one end of a hollow cylinder or frame; and drums with two heads, having heads stretched across both ends of a hollow cylinder or both sides of a circular frame. As developments of the two last-named classes we have drums with jingles and tambourines, and as other forms of instruments with vibrating membranes we have the curious "onion flute" and still more unusual throat horn.

The frame or shell of a drum may be of various materials. Exhibited specimens show drum shells of pottery, metal, wood bent or turned into shape, and logs which are either hollowed to form an open cylinder or scooped out to form a vessel across which the drumhead is stretched. The human skull has been used as the frame and also as the decoration of a drum. The material used for a drumhead also shows a wide variety. Rawhide is a material commonly used by uncivilized peoples, but the skin of the deer, pig, horse, zebra, lizard, and snake appear on drums in this collection; a thin hide resembling parchment is also used, as well as intestines and paper. The method of stretching the head of the drum is an interesting subject and varies with the environment of the people. It is, of course, necessary that the hide be dampened, then fastened in position, after which the drying produces the desired tension. In dry, hot countries the drumhead may be fastened permanently to the shell; but in a moist climate it must be frequently adjusted. The most common method of holding a thin hide in place is by a "flesh hoop," which is used on drums with either one or two heads. Lacings are used in many instances extending from the head (or the flesh hoop) to a ring of heavy rawhide around the base of the drum. Sometimes the two heads are laced together with thongs. The material used for heads on the Chinese drums is very thick and is fastened with two rows of nails driven into the shell. One specimen shows how the head was laced tightly while it was drying, after which it was secured by nails. In many instances the heads are glued to the shells. The heads of drums used by the American Indians are usually fastened in a permanent manner to the frames, and the Indians, in order to increase the tension, hold the drum to the warmth of the fire before using it. This tightens the skin in a short time. Water is sometimes put in a drum to increase the resonance.

The manner of playing the drum shows almost as much variety as the material of which the drum is made. Some drums are beaten with the fingers, the palm, or the whole hand; others with slender rods that strike the entire surface of the head; others with slender sticks that have a curve or loop at the end, while a probable majority are struck with a stick having a knob at the end, this knob being of some soft material. The American Indians secure this by winding the end of the drumstick with rags. In one ceremonial drumstick obtained by the writer the soft end used in striking against the drum was stuffed with eagle feathers. In another drum used in a native religion (the Chippewa Mĭde′wĭwĭn) the end of the stick that touched the drum was frequently carved with a symbolic design. One such stick represented the head of a loon, this bird being associated with certain beliefs of the Mĭde′wĭwĭn. The American Indians select the wood carefully for the drumsticks, the wood of the grapevine and of the hazel being often used.

It is interesting to note the various ways in which drums have been carried, this being mentioned in the descriptions of many specimens. For instance, these drums have been carried on the backs of camels, on the backs of horses, and on the heads and shoulders of men, as well as suspended from the neck and held under the player's arm or in front of him. A few drums are hung on a framework devised for that purpose.

KETTLEDRUMS

This type of drum has a long and interesting history and is the only type which can be tuned to a definite pitch. Some writers claim that the kettledrum was introduced into Europe by the Moors when they occupied Spain. The first drums of this type used in European countries were small. They were always in pairs and strapped around the player's waist. In this form they were used in the triumphal entry of Edward III into Calais in 1347. Kettledrums more nearly the size of those used at the present time were used by German cavalry about the middle of the sixteenth century. They were introduced into England by Henry VIII, who had them played on horseback " after the Hungarian manner." In the time of Charles II every posse of trumpeters had at least one kettledrum. This instrument formed a natural bass to the trumpets, and in the modern orchestra the kettledrum is always associated with the wind instruments. The use of kettledrums in the orchestra began in France in the latter part of the seventeenth century, and they have been more or less permanent members of the orchestra ever since. They are generally used in pairs, one larger than the other, and tuned as a rule to the tonic and dominant. Each drum has a compass of a fifth. The pitch can be raised or lowered by increasing or slackening the tension of the vellum drumhead, this being effected by means of five, six, or even seven screws placed around the circumference of the drum.

A pair of small kettledrums (95146) are from Beirut, Syria. The shells are of yellow brass, bowl shaped, ornamented with respoussé designs of animals, etc. One head of parchment is glued to the shell of each drum. They are beaten with a tapering wooden stick. A particularly interesting kettledrum was received in 1883 from the Rajah of Tagore, India (92726, pl. 24a). The shell is of tinned copper. These drums are tied in a cloth around the waist when played and beaten with the hands. No. 56194 is an Egyptian kettledrum with a shell of thin wood or a section of a gourd. One rawhide head is stretched over the drum and laced from holes made in its edge to a rawhide ring around the base of the shell. The lacing is a rawhide thong; its ends formed into a loop for a handle.

A kettledrum from Calcutta (92726) has a shell of tinned copper and the tension of the head is adjusted by a round patch of black cement placed a little to one side of the center. This drum is called a Banya. The playing of these drums is a difficult art to acquire, but is highly regarded in India. With these is shown a " mescal drum " of the Kiowa Indians, made by stretching a rawhide head on a common iron kettle (169082). The head is held in place by an ingenious arrangement not duplicated in the entire collection.

The largest specimen of kettledrum is from Egypt (56190). It has a shell of beaten copper, 22 inches in diameter and 14 inches high, with a row of heavy metal pins projecting about 2 inches below the rim. The rawhide head is stretched across the drum when wet and held by holes in the edge of the head, passed over the metal pins, and bound by a rawhide thong. Two such drums differing in size are slung across the neck of a camel and carried in religious processions in Cairo, the larger drum on the right side of the camel. The accompanying illustration (pl. 22) was taken at the World's Fair, Chicago, 1893. Another Egyptian kettledrum, one of a pair, is less than 8 inches in diameter and of proportionate height. The shell is of beaten copper. The rawhide or parchment head is laced with rawhide from holes in its edges to a rawhide ring around the base.

A group of interesting drums are of wood, having one head fastened to a shell that is closed at the end opposite the head. The structure may be a solid block of wood in which a resonance chamber has been hollowed, or it may be a shell open at both ends with one end covered by a circle of wood or heavy hide.

A wooden drum of the former type was used by the negroes of Angola in their fetish ceremonies. Three such drums from Africa are shown. No. 18694 is made of a log of red wood and has a mortar-shaped cavity, largest at the upper end. More decorative is 151141, with its shell hollowed from a log of wood and ornamented with a series of bands made of vertical furrows. One rawhide head is laced to pegs driven in the shell. Like all drums of this type it is beaten with the fingers. An interesting drum from Mashonaland in South Africa (167472, pl. 23a) was collected by W. Harvey Browne in 1803. It has one head of zebra skin, pegged to the shell with wooden pins. This type of drum appears as the " voodoo drum " in Haiti. A notable example (292145, pl. 23c) was collected in Haiti by Capt. R. O. Underwood, United States Marine Corps. It is said that in Haiti, the foot of a drum is often embeddied in soft earth so that the drum will stand upright. The shape of this drum suggests that it may have been used in this manner.

A large specimen of this type of drum is from the Sandwich Islands (93607, pl. 23b). The shell is hollowed out of a solid log of Koa wood and is very heavy. The base of the resonance chamber does not rest on the ground but is supported by 10 festoons of open loops cut in the wood. The head of pigskin is fastened without a hoop, numerous holes being made in the edge of the head and lacing passed between these holes and the open loops at the base of the shell. A little red Chinese drum (54034) came from Canton. The shell is turned from a block of wood and beveled at the base. The open top is covered with pigskin fastened with large headed iron nails.

An interesting specimen from the American Indians is 204969, which was used in the Mide'wiwin (Grand Medicine Society) of the Chippewa Indians. The shell of this drum is made from a log of wood hollowed by charring and scraping. It has a wooden bottom, made water-tight with gum or resin. When in use the drum is partly filled with water, which increases its resonance. Such a drum has been heard a distance of 12 miles across a lake. The drumhead is of deerskin, held by a hoop wound with cloth. The head is dampened, laid over the top of the drum, and pressed down by the hoop. As the hide dries it tightens. The tension can be adjusted by moistening the head and holding it in the warmth of a fire. The drumstick is an important adjunct of this ceremonial drum and the end which touches the drum is sometimes carved in a symbolic design. The stick with this drum has a crossbar at the end.

An interesting pair of small kettledrums from Ceylon (95170, pl. 27g) were obtained at the World's Columbian Exposition in Chicago, 1893. The two shells are of conoidal form made from blocks of wood and lashed together side by side. Each has a raw-hide head stretched over a flesh hoop of twisted thongs and laced with a strap from the head to a rawhide ring made of thongs around the base. The rattan drumsticks with hoop-shaped heads are wound with strips of cloth. The larger drum has a shield, or ring-shaped piece about an inch wide, put over the head.

Students of music will be interested in two characteristic drums of India which have the tension of the head regulated by means of wooden "spools." There are the tabla and the mridanga, having, respectively, one and two heads. The tabla (92727, pl. 24d) is turned from a solid block of wood and has its greatest diameter a short distance above the base. The parchment head is laced with thongs to a small rawhide hoop around the base, and crowded under this lacing are eight short cylinders of wood which can be rolled back and forth, adjusting the tension of the head. A round patch of black cement, said to be made of resin and oil, is placed in the center of the head. The reason for this is not explained, but it probably affects both the resonance and the pitch. The pale green margin around the edge of the head of this and the mridanga is not part of the head but a sort of circular mat placed over the parchment and fastened with it to the hoop. Among instrumental performers this and the mridanga are considered the standard instruments and all others are tuned to them.

The mridanga, as mentioned, has two heads, but will be described at this time for comparison with the tabla. The specimen exhibited (92724, pl. 24b) is from Calcutta and is 21½ inches in height. The parchment heads are fastened to hoops which are laced together with thongs. The heads are of different sizes, the larger or bass head being 7½ inches, and the smaller or tenor head being 6½ inches in diameter. The circular spot of black cement is seen on the smaller (tenor) head. According to Albert A. Stanley:[10]

The tension is so regulated, by wooden rollers under the straps, that the two heads are a fourth or a fifth apart in pitch. The larger head is beaten with the left hand, the smaller with the palm, finger tips, and wrist of the right.

Tagore says:

Of all the instruments mridanga, the father of Indian drums, appears to have been the most primitive with respect to its origin. * * * When Mohedeva elated with his victory over the invinc ble demon Tripurasura began to dance, surrounded by Indra and other deities, Brahma is said to have invented the mridanga to serve as an accompaniment.

The instrument is used to accompany dignified music, often in connection with the vina. Capt. Meadows Taylor writes that "On this instrument players are exceedingly expert. * * * The notes which are produced assist the voice, while the time. however complicated, is kept with exactness."

In this section are included drums with shells of earthenware, resembling jars or bowls, and drums made from a chunk of wood, the resonance chamber being hollowed out and a vibrating membrane stretched across the opening. Perhaps the most interesting

[10] Catalogue Stearns Collection at Ann Arbor, Mich., p. 59.

example of the former type is the pottery drum of the Zuni Indians. A particularly fine specimen of this drum is exhibited. Attention is directed to the shape of the rim, which is different from that of an ordinary water jar, permitting a secure fastening of the top. Such drums were used ceremonially and were beaten with sticks having a hoop at the end which touched the drum.

The use of pottery drum shells was general throughout Central America in ancient times as well as more recently in Mediterranean countries, but a majority of the specimens are vase shaped, open at the lower end. From Egypt, however, we have a drum (95698, pl. 25d), consisting of a pottery cup or jar with a rawhide head stretched over the opening and secured by a thong. Two specimens from Morocco are double drums of pottery without the heads. The smaller is 95755 and the larger (95733), consists of two earthenware vessels which resemble kettledrums and are fastened together. They are of the same height, but different diameters, and are decorated with lines etched in the clay. Each had a head of rawhide laced with a thong to a hoop at the base of the shell.

A second type of this class of drums comprises those with shells open at both ends, the lower opening being covered with wood or heavy hide. Two Chinese drums illustrate this structure. The smaller is 94853, which has a shell of thick turned wood, the upper portion rounded and the lower edge beveled with an opening about 4 inches in diameter, which is covered by a circle of heavy hide nailed in position. Near this is a larger Chinese drum with a flat top (54035, pl. 28e). A circle of wood is nailed over the lower, smaller end of the shell. The head of this drum appears to be of horsehide, and shows the holes by which it was stretched while drying. The drum is provided with rings for suspension in a frame and was used in connection with theatrical performances.

DRUMS WITH ONE HEAD

The three general types in this class are the " vase-shaped " drums made of pottery, metal, and wood, the tall slender drums of bamboo and wood, and the hoop with a vibrating membrane stretched across one opening, the latter being a type commonly used by the American Indians.

Vase-shaped drums of pottery with one head have been used for centuries in Central America. Two very rare specimens from the United States of Colombia are in the present collection. They were taken from excavations near Chiriqui and are of gray clay, slender, and resembling a vase. A flaring trumpet-shaped mouth characterizes 109601. The head of this drum was evidently held in place by forcing the parchment into a shallow groove and securing it with a thong. The head of the other Central American specimen (115353) was held by irregular lines cut in the clay. A cord is molded in the clay near the top and around the base.

Several drums with shells of pottery were received in 1889 from Tangiers, Morocco. Their shape is not unlike that of the Central American specimens. No. 95755 (pl. 25a) has a shell of cream-colored ware, glazed on the outside and decorated with designs in blue under the glaze. It has two gut cords vibrating as a "snare" against the head. These were stretched across the top of the shell before the head was put on and were fastened to a leather band which had been placed around the shell. A loop in the leather band forms a handle by which the drum could be carried. Red is the foundation color in the decoration of 95754 (pl. 25f). A striking decoration in warm orange and blue is seen on 95753, while 95750 has a trumpet-shaped mouth and both shell and head are painted in water colors. A particularly fine drum from Morocco is green with a beautifully glazed surface (311649). This was a bequest from Miss Elizabeth S. Stevens. An Arabian specimen of the same type has a different feeling in its decoration, which consists of crude flowers on a background of chrome yellow (151844).

A notable example of pottery vase drum is 95169 from Cairo. This is called Daraboukkeh (according to Mahillon) and is used by boatmen. It is suspended from the player's neck by a cord, held under the left arm, and struck with the fingers of both hands. This is the type of drum used by one of the Egyptian players in a group photographed at the World's Fair, Chicago (pl. 26). A different sound is produced when it is struck in the center and near the edge of the head. This specimen has a bulbous body and long cylindrical neck. The head is glued to the shell, which is open from end to end. Somewhat similar in shape is 95699 (pl. 25c) which is from Constantinople and is the tallest of the pottery drums. The head is stretched over the larger end of the shell and secured by a thong wound several times around the shell. No. 95147 (pl. 25g) is Syrian and shows a somewhat different outline. Attention is directed to the manner in which the parchment head was stretched and held in place while the glue was drying.

Vase-shaped drums of metal and wood are also shown. A particularly fine specimen (95700) is from Turkey and resembles the Syrian pottery drum (95147), but is more graceful in outline. The shell is of brass with repoussé designs of animals, birds, and the ass-headed god. It has one parchment head glued to the shell and made secure by a cord. Another specimen from Turkey is 125883 (pl. 25e). The musicians of Siam used drums of a similar shape, two exhibited specimens coming from that country. No. 27307 (pl.

25b) from Bankok, Siam, has one head of snakeskin stretched over the large end of the shell without a hoop. It is closely laced with split rattan to a slender rattan hoop around the shoulders. The shell is gilded and decorated with small pieces of stained glass and mirror glass fairly encrusting the surface. It is struck with the fingers and palms of both hands. A drum of similar form (96579) was collected in Trong, lower Siam.

An elaborate specimen of this type of drum is 95504, from Rangoon, British Burma. It has a shell shaped like a huge goblet, a portion of which is covered with a green velvet case dotted with spangles. Over this is a flounce of pink cambric bordered with silver braid. The stem and base of the shell are decorated with designs in low relief, gilded and inlaid with bits of mirror and colored glass. This instrument was played by traveling minstrels at Buddhist feasts and, in the days of Buddhist kings, at the reception of the nobles.

Drums open at one end and having one head were made of bamboo, and four such specimens from Java were obtained during the World's Columbian Exposition in 1893. Such a drum consists of a section of bamboo with the septums removed and a rawhide head fastened over one of the open ends. No. 95659 is elaborately decorated with designs consisting of charred lines, while 95600 has a braided band of black and natural colored split rattan around the middle of the shell. The rawhide head of 95658 is laced with rattan to a hoop or band of rattan around the shell. This band is held in place by small wedges driven between the band and the shell of the drum.

Two wooden drums of somewhat similar shape are from Costa Rica, Central America. It is interesting to note the structure of 15413. The head of this drum is the skin of the Iguana lizard, cemented to the shell with fresh blood and held by a wrapping of cord until it dries. This is a favorite instrument of music with the natives and is held under the left arm, suspended by a cord over the shoulder and beaten with the fingers of the right hand. No. 15415 is similar, but made of lighter wood. Both are hollow from end to end like the bamboo drums.

A Malay drum from Singapore (95064, pl. 27c) is shaped like a cannon with a bell-shaped base. One rawhide head is laced back and forth with split rattan to a hoop of twisted rattan wound with brown fiber. This hoop is held in place by wedges driven between it and the shell. Attention is directed to the triangular piece of the drumhead turned upward to form a handle for carrying the drum. Similar in shape and larger in size is 95063, which has a head of lizard skin. The same general proportions appear in a drum used by freed slaves from East Africa living on the Seychelles

Islands (167430). This specimen is 44½ inches in height and 8½ inches in diameter. The shell is made of the trunk of a palm tree and the head is of shark skin, fastened to the shell with small pegs.

Two interesting specimens have shells in the shape of an hourglass, somewhat modified. These are from New Guinea and are unique in that each has a handle midway its length. Excellent workmanship is seen in 125558, which appears to be a modern instrument. The shell is carved from a log of wood, painted black, and ornamented with bands of incised lines filled with white pigment. The lower end is formed like the open jaws of an alligator. No. 73375 (pl. 27e) is a very old instrument and primitive in construction. A wooden handle extends up and down the drum, and on the opposite side is a long rib perforated with small holes in which are tied nutshells, tufts of colored glass, etc. Each drum has a head of lizard skin, glued to the shell.

Four particularly tall drums from Africa are at the rear of the case. These, like the preceding, have one head and a shell that is open from end to end. One of these (151584) is a modern drum from East Africa, received in 1890, while another (95155, pl. 27f) is from West Africa and has a shell hollowed from a log of wood, decorated with carvings and colors. The black is produced by charring, the red is a paint or stain, and the white is clay. It has an openwork base. These drums are used to accompany songs during dances, and are beaten only with the hands. Frequently they are played in connection with horns made of elephant ivory. No. 167499 is made of a hollow log, with one head pegged to the shell with wooden pins.

Two drums from Singapore on the Malay Peninsula resemble those just described in having one head and a shell open at both ends, but are entirely different in their proportions. The diameter of these drums is greater than the height, thus the diameter of 96451 is 14 inches and its height is only 7 inches. The shell is thin and it has a rawhide head stretched over its larger end, held with a hoop of braided split rattan. The lacing of split rattan passes up and down the shell in double rows about 1¼ inches apart, extending from the head to a hoop near the lower end. The lacing is made taut by crowding a stick between the hoop and the lower edge of the shell. A smaller drum of this type is exhibited on a light standard. These instruments are used at marriage feasts and festivals, and are placed on the ground, the player squatting beside the drum and beating it with his open palms.

Exhibited against the wall is the largest single-headed drum in the collection (95708). It is from Ceylon and has a diameter of almost 37 inches. When this is played, several persons sit on the ground in a circle, the back edge of the drum resting on their knees. They strike the drum with their fingers.

A Chinese drum used by Buddhists in their religious ceremonies is 54042, which is beaten with the hands. It is shallow, and the inside flares like the mouth of a trumpet. A somewhat similar drum is the Rumana, from Siam (54078). The shell is of turned wood like the capitol of a Tuscan column. It has three sections of ivory alternating with three of wood in its back edge. An interesting toy drum from China (54037) is made of a section of bamboo painted red. The pigskin head is nailed to the shell with brass-headed nails. An Egyptian hand drum (95165) has a parchment head glued to the shell and is played with two drumsticks.

On the floor of the case are three drums which are open at one end and have one head with a remarkably small vibrating surface. They are played with a slender stick. No. 95854 has a head with a vibrating surface of only 1⅝ inches. The heavy shell is turned from a block of wood and is 7 inches wide at the base and 4¼ inches in height. The inside is flaring like the mouth of a trumpet. The head is stretched over the outside of the shell and nailed with two rows of large-headed iron nails. Another drum of this type from China is 54050. The shell is made of four sections of wood and the head has a vibrating surface of 2 inches. A third specimen of the same type is from Singapore (94916) and consists of a thick ring of wood bound with an iron hoop. The shell is 7 inches in diameter and the vibrating surface of the head is 4¾ inches.

A hand drum with one head is used extensively by the American Indians. This usually consists of a wooden hoop, 11 to 18 inches or more in diameter, with a cover of rawhide, either fastened to the hoop or stretched over it with the corners (or thongs tied to the corners) crossed on the reverse side of the drum as a handhold. An example of this instrument is 64346.

An interesting drum from the Aleuts on Commander Island, Alaska, is 73020, obtained in 1882 or 1883. It has an oval shell, made of a hoop, the joint lapped and nailed. A handle fits over the joint and is nailed with wire nails. The head is made of the bladder of a fur seal. It is stretched over the hoop when green and held by being forced into a groove, made in the outside of the hoop, by means of a cord. A twisted sinew cord is passed four times across the head, acting as a snare.

From the Tlingits at Sitka, Alaska, we have 20732, purchased in 1875. The shell is a bent hoop of pine. The rawhide or thin skin head is stretched over the hoop when green and fastened to the back edge of the hoop with wooden pins. Two rawhide thongs are stretched across the back of the hoop so as to cross at the middle.

Two Eskimo drums with handles are exhibited, 93875 being from Fort Alexander, Alaska. The shell is 17 by 18½ inches in diameter, and the entire length of the specimen is more than 31 inches. The end of the handle inside the drum is carved to represent a loon's head. The drum has one head supposed to be seals' intestines. This is stretched over the hoop and pressed into a groove by means of a thong wound several times around the hoop. When played, the hoop and not the head is struck by the drumstick. The inside of the hoop is painted in alternate sections of white and red.

An Eskimo drum from the same locality as the preceding is 93877. The handle is 45 inches long, its inner end carved to represent the head and beak of an albatross. The single head is supposed to be made from a whale's bladder. The inside of the head is decorated with a rude pictograph in black representing the hunting of a whale. The back edge of the hoop, not the head, is struck when this drum is played.

Two Tlingit drums from Sitka, Alaska, are 20733 and 74436. The inside of the latter is painted with a conventionalized figure of Hoots, the bear, in red and black.

An interesting Shoshone drum (22013) was the gift of Maj. J. W. Powell. The head is of tanned deerskin, stretched over and inside the hoop and stitched through and through. The face is painted red. Two cords of twisted skin crossing diagonally at the back form a handhold. The head of this type of drum is tightened by holding it near a fire, where it is gradually warmed. Another Shoshone drum (22301) is from Fort Hall. The head is nailed in place with brass-headed nails. On the head is painted in colors an open teepee, etc. A drum of the Yankton Sioux (8390) was received in 1869. The rawhide head is stretched over and round the hoop. Two thongs crossing each other diagonally and their centers passing through a wooden spool form the handhold. All drums of this class are played with a drumstick.

A particularly interesting drum from Zanzibar is 95239. The shell is hollowed from a block of wood, both ends being open. One head of rawhide is closely laced with a leather thong to a cap of rawhide drawn over the base. It is played with a pair of drumsticks. From the lower Congo is 76251 (pl. 27b), which has one head of goatskin laced to a goatskin cap with a large hole in the center, placed over the lower end of the drum.

DRUMS WITH TWO HEADS

An interesting group of double-headed drums from the North American Indians is in the collection. These drums are broad and shallow, and their uses were as varied as the life of the Indians. They accompanied the war songs, were played during dances, and also when games were in progress. Some specimens show the two heads cut from one large hide and stretched in such a manner that the seam extends around only a portion of the rim, while in other specimens the two heads are separate, their edges brought together and stitched in a seam around the entire rim. These drums were beaten with a rather short stick having a padded end. This end was usually formed by winding rags around the end of the stick.

No. 9057 is a Sisseton Sioux (Dakota) drum with hoop of bent wood and two rawhide heads stitched together around the outside of the hoop. It has a clever handle made by slitting the edge of one head and stretching the piece into a loop. The drum is painted red, green, and black, with a four-pointed star on one side. A Tonkawa drum from southern Texas (8453) is painted brown and ornamented with red and green paint. A twisted thong of hide forms a loop handle. The drumstick has a stuffed head of deerskin and its other end is ornamented with a tassel of leather thongs.

An interesting group of double-headed drums from Siam, China, and Japan are cask shaped and have brass-ringed staples by which they were suspended when in use. A royal drum (3946) was given to President Pierce by the King of Siam. The shell is dark wood with a bilge like a cask. Two rawhide heads are nailed to the shell with large brass-headed nails. No. 27257 is similar but a little larger. A particularly large Chinese drum is 54032, which has a length of 23 inches and a maximum diameter of 31 inches. The shell is cask shaped and decorated with a vine and flowers in green on a brown ground. One end is painted black and the other is painted with a dragon and other mythical animals. A notable specimen of this type was given to the Museum in 1876 by the Chinese Imperial Centennial Commission (54040). On the inside of the cask-shaped shell are two steel wires fastened at one end. One wire has its free end bent at a right angle like the tongue of a jew's-harp and the other wire forms a coil around it. These wires make a jingling noise when the drum is disturbed. Such drums are said to have been used in temples consecrated to Confucius. The Buddhist priests of China used a drum in their religious ceremonies, such an instrument being 54047.

A temple drum from Tokio, suspended in a carved frame is 93207. On top of the frame is an ornament in openworked and closed brass which is said to represent the three severed pearls enveloped in flames, called Kwa-yen.

An elaborately decorated drum from Japan is 94666. The shell is painted with designs of dragons and clouds in colors on a golden ground an dthe heads are painted with geometrical designs in colors on a background of gold. The drumstick is lacquered. Another cask-shaped drum from Japan has two characters branded between the ringed staples. The shell is turned from a log of wood and.

as in other drums of this type, the two heads are fastened with nails having large rounded heads.

A small Japanese drum with cask-shaped shell is 261051 (pl. 28*a*), the two rawhide heads nailed to the shell with nails having black rounded heads. A double-headed Chinese drum (96568, pl. 28*d*) is similar in structure to the foregoing but different in proportions, the diameter being greater than the height. A group of toy drums from China are Nos. 54036, 54038, and 54039. A small cask-shaped drum (96578) is from Trong, lower Siam. Each head has a braided hoop of split rattan around it below the nails that fasten the head to the shell. It has a brass staple in the middle of the shell, around which are two copper washers, their edges toothed.

No. 95202 (pl. 28*c*) is Korean, consisting of a shell of wood covered with cloth and paper, painted with two dragons. The designs on the rawhide heads also represent dragons. Like other drums of this sort, it was suspended by two ringed staples when in use.

Two drums in this group have shells of turned wood, 3946 being from Korea and 27318 from Siam. The latter is a common form of Siamese drum, having two rawhide heads laced back and forth with split rattan. This specimen is almost 27 inches long.

Attention is directed to 94665 (pl. 28*b*), which has two heads of paper nailed to the shell with large-headed nails. The shell is of black lacquered wood and the heads are painted with flowers in colors and geometrical designs in black. It is described as " Taiko antique temple drum 1650."

The collection contains several double-headed drums with shell hollowed from a log.

A curious little drum from Baranquilla, State of Bolivar in Colombia, probably has an interesting history (95542). The shell is hollowed from an irregular log of wood. Holes are made through the heads for the lacing, which is twisted cord. A double cord is passed over one head, forming a snare. A Malay drum of this type is 216282 (pl. 27*d*), collected by Dr. W. L. Abbott. The shell, hollowed from a log of hard redwood, is a little larger at one end than the other. The two heads are laced back and forth, the tension increased by four bands of split rattan which draw the lacings together in squares.

An interesting Hopi drum (22478, pl. 27*a*) was received from Maj. J. W. Powell in 1875. The shell is a section of a hollow irregular log with the bark removed. Two heads of rawhide, probably goat, are stretched over the ends of the shell without hoops and laced with a thong of rawhide through holes made in the edges of the heads, back and forth. The end of this thong is formed into a loop for a handle. The drum is 8¼ inches high and the diameter varies from

7 to 8¼ inches. A "country drum" from Egypt, with shell of bent wood painted black, is 95172.

Several of the double-headed drums are highly decorated. Among these is 95287, a "tenor" or "long drum" from Italy. A Siamese drum (27317) is barrel shaped and larger at one end than the other. It is painted red and stenciled with gilt designs. No. 94664 is from Japan, the cylindrical shell gilded and painted in colors. Two rawhide heads are stretched over hoops of greater diameter than the shell of the drum. The lacing is a thong of rawhide passing back and forth across the shell from holes made in the heads close to the hoops. It rests on a fancy lacquered stand and is played with two drumsticks resembling those for a snare drum.

Another decorated drum is 93211 from Tokio. The shell is gold lacquer with designs of flowers and foliage in raised gold. The outer surface of the heads has a border of black lacquer and the hem on the under side of the heads is gilded. This is held on the right shoulder by the left hand, and struck with the right hand. An imposing Japanese drum (not numbered) is about 54 inches in diameter and decorated with dragons.

A notable specimen from India (54070 pl. 24c), was given to President R. B. Hayes in 1879 by Rajah Sourindro Mohun Tagore, founder and president of the Bengal Music School at Calcutta. The shell is built up of staves, cask shaped, and covered with maroon velvet, the ears ornamented with silk tassels. It is a drawing-room instrument and was beaten by the hands. Another interesting drum from India is 92725. The shell is made from a log of wood and is larger in the middle than at the ends. It has two parchment heads tightened by brass rings on lacings of cord. A drum somewhat similar to this is shown with the group of Hindu musicians (pl. 29).

A peculiar Chinese drum (54045) has a shell which suggests a gigantic dumb-bell. It is 31 inches long and the diameter of the heads is 11 inches. The heads are stretched over hoops made of round iron. Small holes are made in the heads and in each is a brass hook or link by which the heads are laced together. These cords are tightened by means of leather bags or ears.

No. 55732 is a "side or snare drum for boys." The shell is of bent wood veneered with mahogany. The bolter head is of calfskin and the snare head is of sheepskin. The heads are stretched over flesh hoops with tightening hoops and with lacing of brown linen cord. The heads are made taut by means of leather ears.

The tallest drum in the entire collection is 95218, which is 85½ inches high. The shell is largest at the middle of its length and the diameter of one end is more than double that of the other. It is from the French Congo in Africa. On one side is a carved loop handle and below is a bas-relief of an African wrought-iron bell, the insignia of a chief. Below this carving the shell is shaped in seven sides in a spiral around the body. The upper head is of goat or antelope skin stretched over the large end without a hoop, and is laced back and forth with a twisted thong of rawhide to a cap or head of rawhide drawn over the lower end. It is beaten with a short cylindrical stick and is used on festive occasions and at dances to signalize a welcome. When a chief dies these drums are beaten incessantly for weeks or months. Concerning a similar drum, it is said, "When in service the drum is carried on the shoulder of one man while a second walks behind beating it."

A curious Hindu drum (125561) was fastened to the forehead, being held in place by a curved iron plate. It consists of a hoop covered by a parchment head and was beaten with the hands.

DRUMS WITH JINGLES

An Indian drum with jingles set in the frame is an instrument which resembles the tambourine. Such an instrument is 8484. It was collected by Dr. J. P. Kimball, assistant surgeon, United States Army, in 1869, from the Assiniboine Indians at Fort Buford, in Dakota. This was not shaken but beaten with a drumstick, the jingles adding to the sound. These jingles are of brass and are hung in four rectangular holes in the hoop of the drum. The head is of tanned skin tacked to the hoop and painted on the outside with a red dish and on the inside with designs in red, yellow, blue, and black.

A Korean drum with two heads (95622) has a jingle attached to the handle.

TAMBOURINES

The structure of a tambourine is like that of a one-headed drum with jingles set in the frame, but the tambourine is an individual instrument of great antiquity, probably older than the drum. The frames are of three sorts—frames of bent wood, of turned wood, and of sections of wood sawed and fitted into a circular form.

Spain is the country with which the tambourine, like the castanet, is most closely associated and the collection contains two Spanish tambourines. These are of the small size used by professionals who prefer tambourines with heads of goatskin and shells neither painted nor varnished. The frames are of bent wood and the instruments are strongly made, as the professionals often use so much force in their playing that the instruments fly to pieces in their hands. No. 95557 is 6⅛ inches in diameter. The shell is a bent hoop of maple reinforced with three half-round hoops. It is mortised for eight pairs of flat, tin jingles, arranged in four groups of two each. A larger instrument (95558) has 10 pairs of jingles. These specimens have each a round thumb hole in the shell. A tambourine from Morocco (95771) has the shell made of two thicknesses of bent wood, mortised for five pairs of jingles. The parchment head is gaily painted with colored designs on a red ground. This has no thumb hole.

Continuing the series of tambourines with hoops of bent wood, we note two interesting specimens from Egypt, 95167 being the more typical of the two. The hoop is mortised with 10 openings in 2 rows of 5 each, and in each opening is suspended a pair of jingles. The hoop is inlaid with pearl, horn, and light-colored woods. One parchment head was stretched across the hoop when wet and glued in place. The other Egyptian tambourine (56192) is considerably larger. The shell is painted red on the inside and thickly hung with wire chains composed of three circular rings, hung from staples in the wood. The rawhide head almost covers the outside of the shell, to which it is glued.

A curious instrument from Tiflis, Russia (72971), has the inside of the shell painted red and the outside inlaid with bone, horn, and light-colored woods. The inside is hung with 80 jingles pendant from brass staples passing through brass escutcheons. The jingles are brass rings, small bells, and coins or medals, seven rings alternating with three bells or three coins, etc. The parchment head is glued to the shell, its outer edge covered with a ribbon of green parchment nailed with brass nails. A heavy tambourine came from Barbados Island (94874). The hoop is of two thicknesses of bent wood, lapped and nailed and mortised for three pairs of large jingles. The structure is particularly heavy throughout the instrument.

Two American tambourines are shown, and are of about the same size (Nos. 55754 and 55755).

Tambourines from Singapore and Calcutta have shells turned from blocks of wood, 94912 resembling a shallow bowl without a bottom. The head is nailed to the shell, which is hung with three pairs of copper jingles. It was used at marriage feasts and festivals. The tambourine from India (92728, pl. 24e) has only one pair of jingles. The outside of the head is painted with bands of black, yellow, and red with a green edge. According to Tagore, it is a pastoral instrument used by the religious mendicants as an accompaniment to their songs.

The Chinese tambourines in the collection have a shell or hoop made of sections of wood sawed and mortised to form a circle. The shell of 54051 is made of five sections of wood sawed to form a circle and bound with a narrow iron hoop. It has five rectangular holes in the shell and a pair of tin jingles set in each hole. The head is of pigskin, painted with flowers in colors surrounded with a band of arabesques in blue. Another tambourine from China is octagonal and has one snake-skin head and seven pairs of jingles.

ONION FLUTES

The collection contains two forms of musical instruments with vibrating membranes which are not sounded by percussion. The first is an " onion flute," receiving its name from the frequent use of an onion skin as a membrane in its construction. The specimens exhibited (216020 *a* and *b*) are copies of a French instrument which is said to have been in vogue at the beginning of the seventeenth century. Concerts were given in which four or five of these instruments were played. The instrument is sounded by being sung into like a zobo or kazoo. An onion flute is in three sections, the upper one hollow, shaped like an egg, and perforated with small holes. This fits on a tenon 1 inch in diameter which is covered with onion skin, paper, or bladder. The mouth hole is large and is placed 5½ inches below the tissue-covered end of the tube. The instrument has only false finger holes and a slightly flaring bell.

THROAT HORNS

The second form of vibrating membrane not a drum is a Bengalese instrument called "throat horn." A pair of these (5407 *a* and *b*) were obtained from Doctor Tagore in 1879. These are of hammered silver in the shape of an ordinary straight conical horn with a cupped mouthpiece, but instead of being blown they were held against the vocal cords in the throat or the cheek, producing a reedy note. According to Mahillon there is a thin convex disk of metal that fits in the cupped mouthpiece. This is placed in a piece of cocoon skilfully cut and inserted in such a manner as to vibrate, producing a tone.

BASKET USED AS A DRUM

An inverted basket is used as a drum by the Piman and Yuman Tribes of American Indians. The basket thus used is a household article, an excellent example being 217885, collected by Russell. Among the Papago this basket is struck with the palm of the hand except in a certain class of ceremonial songs in which it is rubbed downward with a short flat stick. The usual procedure is to drop the basket on the ground wrong side up in such a manner as to produce an explosive sound. The players then seat themselves around it. If two men are playing they may strike it with both hands, but more frequently there are four players each striking it with his right hand as he sings. The Yuma Indians strike the basket with willow drumsticks or with bundles of arrow weed, each form of accompaniment being used with certain sorts of songs.

These appliances for striking the drum are not held in the usual manner, one in each hand, but the two sticks or bundles are both held in the same hand, side by side. Specimens of these (235190 and 325189) were seen in use and collected by the writer.

SECTION 4. STRINGED INSTRUMENTS

The pleasing sound of a string, stretched and plucked with the fingers or struck with a rod, was among the early discoveries of the human race in the field of esthetics. Next came a knowledge that the resonance of the tone was increased if the string were stretched over something hollow, as a gourd or hollow block of wood. Since one string gave a pleasing sound, why should not two strings give more pleasure, especially if they were different in length and pitch? On these two sensations of pleasure the whole history of stringed instruments is founded. In the following section, and by means of exhibited instruments, we will follow this interesting history from the musical bow and the one-stringed instrument of oriental and Asiatic countries, through the lyre and lute to the mandolin, guitar, and violin, and through the harp, psaltery, and dulcimer, to the clavicord and harpsichord, and finally to the pianoforte of the present day. Such a marvelous development must of necessity be gradual. An entire generation might pass without producing a single inventive mind that would improve the existing form of stringed instrument. In the next generation it might occur to some one to devise a new way of regulating the tension of the string or increasing the resonance. Such a device, once found to be successful, was handed down as an improvement in the instrument and became a factor in its further development. Such a device, for instance, was the tuning peg set in a rigid bar. Previous to that device the tension of the string was determined by the point at which it was attached to a flexible rod. Another great advance was made by the man who in the remote past substituted animal for vegetable material in strings. Across the years we greet these long-forgotten lovers of music whose individual effort carried their instrument a little farther toward efficiency and excellence of tone production.

INSTRUMENTS WITH OPEN STRINGS, PICKED

Probably no musical instrument has a wider distribution than the musical bow. According to Balfour, it is found throughout southern Africa, in India, the Malay Islands, Mexico, and Patagonia, and there are traditions of its use in central Brazil and Japan. Opinions differ as to the explanation of its presence in the Western Hemisphere.

The musical bow is the simplest stringed instrument, and is briefly described as a flexible stick with a string stretched between the two ends. According to tradition, the archer's bow was temporarily used as a musical instrument and then developed in a variety of forms for musical use. In its earliest period the bow was held against the player's lips, the mouth acting as a resonator when, the string was struck or twanged by the fingers. Such a specimen in the exhibit has a particularly interesting history (95201, pl. 30a). The bow is of oak, about 26 inches long, and the string is of steel wire. Beside it will be seen the twisted wire with which it was twanged. Prof. Otis T. Mason writes that a native Zulu negro came into his office one day carrying this instrument, which he played in the following manner: The bow was held in his left hand with the back against his lip, thus allowing his capacious mouth to act as a resonator. In his right hand he held a piece of twisted wire about 9 inches long, and he struck this against the string of the bow in rapid strokes, the wire touching the bow with both the upward and downward motions. He varied the sound by changing the shape of the cavity of his mouth, after the manner of a player on the jew's-harp. Mr. Hawley states that "the maker and player, Unger Sibassio, produced five notes, if not an octave, on this instrument." Three other specimens show a single cord fastened to a bow, but have a peg by which the string is tightened. Such a specimen is 48049, from San Ildefonso, in New Mexico, collected by James Stevenson in 1880. One end of the string is fastened to the bow and the other to the small end of a tuning peg. No. 19687 is from Indians living on the Tule River in California and was received in 1875. It is made from a cornstalk and has one string of twisted sheep gut. The stalk shows a hole for a tuning peg, which is not with the specimen. A still older specimen is 48048 (pl. 30b), collected among the Yaqui of Sonora, Mexico, by Palmer in 1869. This is made of cane and has one string of sheep's gut fastened to a transverse tuning peg.

The musical bows already described were played as open strings. From Mashonaland, South Africa, we have an instrument (167516), which is equally simple in construction but played as a stopped string. The bow is a piece of cane, slightly curved. It has one slender string of gut. The player holds the upper end of the bow in his teeth and picks the string with his right thumb, stopping the string against the bow with the index finger of his left hand. From the same locality we have 167517, an instrument of more elaborate construction with what might be regarded as a rudimentary bridge. A cord is tied from the string to the back of the bow, bending the string toward the bow and dividing it into two unequal parts, which produce two open tones. It will be noted that the musical bows thus far described are without resonators. The first actual development consisted in attaching a portion of a gourd to the bow as a resonator.

This was attached loosely, and the vibrating length of the string was regulated by slipping the gourd along the rod. The gourd resonator of the musical bow was pressed against the player's abdomen. The string was struck with a small bamboo and the tone varied by moving the fingers along the string and by inclining the gourd at different angles, varying the open space between the player's body and the open edge of the gourd. These instruments vary in length from 1 to 7 or more feet, and the strings, which are one to six in number, could be played either open or stopped. The sound was produced in various ways, the strings being picked by the fingers or a plectrum, rubbed, or struck with a beater.

No. 94661 has one string of twisted cord and a gourd resonator which is tied to the bow and pressed against the naked body of the player, as shown in Plate 31. It was struck with a stick having a ball at the end, this ball consisting of a plant substance tied in a cloth and having loose seeds that rattle when the stick is shaken. The material used as a string is a vine or root, and a roll of this is shown 95163 (pl. 30g). The roll contains two coils, one finer than the other and each about 60 feet long. There is something appealing in the thought of the native musician who put a supply of extra strings with his instrument. On 151140 (pl. 30c) is seen about two-thirds of a spherical gourd as a bell-shaped resonator, loosely tied to the bow. No. 167477 is similar and has a string of rolled rawhide, and 95926 has a string of vegetable fiber in two strands twisted together. The resonator of each is made from a gourd shell. W. L. Abbott, who collected the specimens, says: "The bow is strung taut and held in the left hand with the hollow of the gourd pressed against the player's chest. The string is struck with a small stick held in the player's right hand." A section of a long gourd serves as a resonator on 167515, being fastened to the bow at one side near the middle. It is struck with a bamboo rod.

A musical bow with four strings and a bridge is seen as 95159 from the Gaboon River in West Africa. This type is called a muet. The bow is made from the stalk of a palm leaf. Four strings of different lengths are cut from the cuticle of the palm leaf, one end of each being left attached. They are stretched across an upright wooden bridge and held by vertical notches about half an inch apart. The strings were tuned by moving back and forth two braided bands which were placed at the ends of the bow. Mr. Hawley says that the strings on the long end are tuned D, G, A, B. Half of a gourd shell is tied to the back of the bow opposite the bridge as a resonator. The strings were picked with the fingers. As an accompaniment to this stringed instrument the natives played a percussion instrument consisting of a piece of bamboo about 40 inches long. This was laid across the knees of two performers seated on stools and each pounded it with a pair of drumsticks (95158). No. 95160 is more than 53 inches long and has four strings and a gourd resonator, but lacks the bridge described with the preceding specimen.

The muet is followed, in point of development, by the lyre. A majority of the primitive lyres in the exhibition cases are from Africa. Two specimens show the use of five strings without tuning pegs, one of these (76250, pl. 41*f*) acquired by the Museum in 1885, is particularly crude as it contains no metal. The thin top appears to be a planed board, but the remainder of the instrument shows no mark of a tool other than a sharp knife. There are no sound holes in the top, but a space is left open at the end. The projection of the top beyond the body affords additional resonance space as well as a brace for the thumb while the fingers twang the strings. Five sticks are inserted in the end of the body of the instrument and are bent upward by removing the bark on the inner side of the curve. The strings consist of two strands of grass root twisted together. They are inserted in the body of the instrument and the free ends secured to the curved sticks at an angle above the body of the instrument. The tuning of the strings was accomplished by sliding the fastening up and down the curved stick, the elasticity of the stick providing a tension that affects the pitch. Another lyre resembles this, but is less crude (95806). The entire end is open and remotely suggests half a violin. The strings are apparently of the same material as in the specimen last described, but the root fiber is used in a single instead of a double strand. Attention is directed to the loop of fiber by which the instrument was carried.

Two African lyres have the strings tightened by a cylindrical bit of wood placed beneath them at the point where they are inserted in the instrument. No metal was used in 95224, the top being held in place by wooden pegs and the strings being vegetable fiber. The entire surface of the body has been charred and scraped, after which the outer surface was removed in a pattern showing the natural color of the wood. The same structure is seen in 95225, but the wood appears to have been "rubbed down" smoothly after charring and the incised lines filled with white pigment. A human head, roughly carved, projects from the upper end of the body.

Four lyres have bodies covered with hide, and strings attached to tuning pegs. The only Egyptian instrument in this group is 95179 (pl. 41*g*), which is made of a block of wood, the inside hollowed out like a trough. A stick serving for the neck of the instrument is inserted in one end. The entire block is covered with rawhide, evidently put on when green, fitted smoothly to the wood and sewed up the back. Two sound holes are cut in the top. Before the rawhide was put in place five gut strings were threaded through it in a longitudinal row and attached to a narrow strip of wood on the under side. After the rawhide had dried the free ends of the strings were attached to tuning pegs in the neck of the instrument, and their various lengths probably produced differences in pitch. The strings were plucked by the fingers. A somewhat similar construction is seen in 174757 (pl. 32a), but this instrument has an elliptical body with a rounded back, and the neck turns sharply upward about 4 inches from the body. The five strings are of grass or vegetable fiber. An ambitious design appears in 95161 and 95162. The neck projects sharply upward and beneath it is carved a human head. One instrument is covered with antelope hide having the hair on it. These instruments are from the Gaboon River in West Africa. It is said, " formerly this instrument was played only during the ceremony of initiation into the mysteries of the Bieti. Now they are played at any time." Probably no person living at the present time can describe from personal knowledge the strange rites with which this particular specimen was associated in the wilds of Africa. An Egyptian lyre (95137, pl. 32b) has eight strings of twisted gut.

A lyre from Senegambia (96842) has a body consisting of half a gourd shell with a rawhide belly. A large triangular sound hole is made in one side of the gourd shell. It has 10 strings of material that looks like some sort of vine. The bridge is a thin piece of wood, placed almost upright. The strings are wound several times around the neck and tied, and are tuned by sliding upward and downward the coils placed around the neck of the instrument.

The design of 14260 is remotely suggestive of a triangular harp. The base is a portion of a spherical gourd and above it is a triangular frame of sticks. It probably had seven strings of vegetable fiber of graduated lengths running from the upright to the diagonal standard, parallel to the spreader which extends between them.

An Ethiopian lyre of different outline is the kissar (95178, pl. 41c), which resembles the Hebrew kinnor and the Greek kithara or lyre. Representations of this type of instrument are seen on ancient Egyptian and Assyrian monuments, small forms of it being carried in processions. The kissar has a body resembling a very shallow bowl. The belly of rawhide is secured by lacing to a coil or loop on the back of the instrument. Two posts, set in the back of the instrument, diverge and are united by a crossbar at the top. Between the posts is a string of shells. The five strings are of camel gut and are tuned by turning the cloth rings on the crossbar. Engel states that the strings are vibrated alternately by the fingers and by a horn plectrum.

Musical instruments with one string are akin to the musical bow of primitive people. The collection contains numerous specimens

of these instruments, some of which are noted in special groups, as
the one-stringed koto (96840, pl. 30*f*) is described with the other
koto on page 86. One of the most interesting is the eka-tara of India
(92705, pl. 30*d*), an instrument used by religious mendicants to accompany their songs. The bamboo neck of this instrument passes
entirely through the gourd body, which has a belly of parchment.
The string is tied to the short end of the bamboo, passed over a bridge
on the body of the instrument, and tuned by a peg on the longer
end of the bamboo. The bridge is a simple arch with a notch at the
crown for the string. Two other musical instruments from India
have one gut string passed through a membrane which is stretched
across the bottom of a hollow block of wood. Thence the string
passes upward, and in one specimen (92702) it was held in the hand
while in the other (92706) it was attached to a tuning peg in the
uncut portion of a bamboo cane which formed the upper part of the
instrument. This cane was split and one of its prongs attached to
each side of the block of wood, the shape of the whole being somewhat like that of a bucket with a long, stiff handle. Mahillon, describing the first-named instrument, says that the end of the string
is usually fastened to a small cocoanut shell. " The player holds the
instrument loosely between his arm and side, his hand grasping
the cocoanut shell and stretching the string, varying its tension.
* * * He strikes the string with a wooden plectrum in his other
hand. This is used principally by the singing beggars." The second-
named instrument has a wire string and was used by religious
mendicants for accompanying pastoral songs.

The primitive stringed instrument 94642 (pl. 30*e*) was received at
a very early date and its history is unknown. It has one string of
twisted fiber and apparently was played with a bow consisting of a
slender stick strung with a bundle of natural fiber. With this group
is a one-stringed fiddle of the Apache Indians (21536, pl. 30*h*).

The harp is of great antiquity, being the first musical instrument mentioned in the Bible (Genesis iv, 21). It was the special
instrument of David and later was one of the most important members of the temple orchestra, but its form in early times is said to
have resembled the Greek lyre instead of the triangular harp with
which we are familiar.

It is not difficult to trace the development of the harp from the
musical bow. We have noted the addition of a gourd resonator
to the ordinary hunting bow, then the use of a hollowed block of
wood as a resonator and the addition of several strings, this stage
of development being represented by the African lyre. Next we
have the Burmese harps, with strings attached to a curved arm
that extends over the sound box. Imagine this curved arm leaving
the sound box at a sharp angle (like the top of the modern harp),

then imagine a pillar connecting the end of the arm with the sound box, and we have the structure of the triangular harp.

The Burmese harps were held in the lap when played, with the neck toward the left. Both hands were used to pluck the strings, and occasionally the left hand was laid across the neck of the instrument, stopping the strings. No. 175190 has six strings of graduated lengths tuned by transverse pegs. Another instrument (95490, pl. 32c) is tuned like the primitive African lyres by slipping the string up and down on the neck. This harp was played at marriages and at the boring of children's ears. In the days of the Burmese kings it was played for the amusement of royalty before retiring.

The characteristic of the harp previous to the eighteenth century was that each string produced only one tone, though makers of the guitar had learned long before that time to produce many tones by stopping the strings, and therefore were able to reduce the length and number of the strings. No. 95258 is a Neapolitan diatonic harp said to have been made about the year 1600. Comparison with the magnificent specimen No. 324705 will show that the earlier harp lacks the pedals which make possible the production of three tones from each string. The Neapolitan harp exhibited had originally 36 strings of lengths graduated from 3 to 47 inches, and is typical of the medieval harp.

The pedal mechanism of the modern harp was preceded by a device consisting of little crooks of metal screwed into the neck. These could be turned against the strings, shortening them and raising the pitch a semitone. The invention of the pedal mechanism is generally credited to Hochbrucker, of Bavaria, about the year 1720, and the perfecting of the mechanism was accomplished by Erard in the early years of the nineteenth century. No. 95327 (pl. 32d) is a single-action harp made by Erard, probably before 1810, the year in which he brought out his double-action harp. It is called a "lap harp chromatici." The pitch is affected by four thumb keys, whose action is, in part, described by Upham as follows: "If the strings are tuned in the diatonic scale from c (second space base clef) to f (fifth line treble clef) then turning the first thumb key would sharpen all the Fs of the different octaves, giving the key of G major; turning the first and third keys would sharpen all the Fs and Cs, giving the key of D major," etc. The double action with its pedal mechanism, perfected in 1810 by Erard, makes it possible to raise the pitch of any group of strings a whole tone. The harp of the present time has a compass of 6½ octaves, 47 strings, and 7 pedals and is tuned to the scale of C flat. The harpist uses both hands in playing, and the music is written on treble and bass staves, the same as for the piano.

With this group is classified the auto harp (95237), whose strings are sounded by the manipulation of a series of bars.

INSTRUMENTS WITH STOPPED STRINGS, PICKED

Some of the most ancient instruments of oriental races belong to this group, as well as the medieval lute and the modern guitar, banjo, zither, and mandolin. Confucius, the Chinese philosopher, was so fond of a certain musical instrument that it was called the lyre of Confucius. It is now called the "scholar's lute" (54023, pl. 33c). Another ancient Chinese instrument of this class is the "moon guitar," two specimens of which are exhibited (95729 and 13044). The "tamboura" (or tanboura) is one of the simplest and most ancient of these instruments, and was known to the Assyrians and Egyptians 3,000 years ago. An Egyptian tamboura is 95244, while 95312 is a small tamboura from Turkey, its sound hole filled with an openwork parchment rosette. A large tamboura from Cairo (95175) is strung with three brass and five steel strings, passed over a bridge of dark redwood. It has 17 frets of gut wound around the finger board. The "nofre," almost identical in construction, had a very long neck, two or four strings, and was often provided with frets consisting of cord wound around the neck of the instrument at carefully calculated distances. This instrument shows that the Egyptians at an early date had learned to produce on a few strings, by means of a fretted finger board, a larger number of tones than was obtainable on the harp. The influence of the nofre and tamboura is seen in the lute and mandolin with pear-shaped bodies and in the guitar with its flat back, also in the banjo. It will be noted that all these instruments have vibrating, plucked strings passed over frets or bridges.

The lute is an instrument with a body shaped like half a pear, and it is especially traced in ancient India, Persia, and countries influenced by their civilization. It always had a round sound hole, and usually had both open and stopped strings and frets on the finger board that gave semitones. The peg box is always at an angle with the neck. The various forms of its name suggest that it passed from Arabia and Egypt into northern Africa and was carried by the Moors into Spain, whence it spread over all Europe. The medieval lute flourished during the period of creative Gothic architecture, subsided as the violin quartet arose, and became obsolete with the coming of the pianoforte. Originally the lute had four strings, but others were added in course of time. They were picked either with the fingers or with a quill. The medieval lute was so hard to keep in tune that Matheson said, "A luterist 80 years old has certainly spent 60 years in tuning his instrument." The oldest instrumental compositions we possess were written for the lute and organ, the notation for the lute being a special system known as tablature.

The group of old Italian lutes is particularly interesting. The bass double-necked lute, called "chitarroni" (95252), was made by Augustius Costa, of Brescia, in 1622. It is 77⅝ inches long and has five gut frets tied around the neck and finger board. It is strung with 11 gut strings, part of which do not pass over the finger board, but are tuned by transverse pegs set in a second neck. The vibrating length of the stopped strings (over the finger board) is 30 inches, while that of the open strings is 62¾ inches. The use of the long, open bass strings points to a time prior to the knowledge that the pitch of a string could be lowered by winding it closely with wire. Such strings are said to have been introduced in France in 1625, and are known as "overspun" or "silver" strings. A smaller instrument of this type is 95250.

A different type of bass lute is the theorbo (95306), made about 1600. This differs from the arch lute, or arciliuto (95308, pl. 34c) only in the tuning of the stopped strings, which in the former are tuned singly and in the latter are tuned in pairs. An engraved pearl plate on the liuto (95255) bears an inscription, which is translated "Giovanni, son of Giuseppe Gerusa, 1761," indicating the name of the maker and date of manufacture.

The Italian mandola, or lute-shaped cither, had the form of a lute, but was smaller. A particularly fine instrument, dated 1661, is 95254 (pl. 34e).

A modern Arabian lute is shown as 125556 (pl. 34a). The finger board is inlaid with ivory and pearl and has no frets. The Syrian lute, 95143, has no frets and has 12 gut strings tuned in pairs. It is picked with a long piece of quill stripped from the staff of a black feather. A modern Egyptian lute (125557) has its head terminating with the carved neck and head of a peacock. It has 12 strings. A Moorish lute from Tangiers is shown as 95736. The finger board is inlaid with bone and pearl and it has no frets. It is strung with eight gut strings tuned in pairs. Over the lower end is a shield or protector of gold-embroidered velvet.

A particularly handsome specimen is the lute from Arabia (125556). The body is built up of 11 bent staves of thin wood and the belly is of thin unvarnished pine. The neck is half round, its back inlaid with vines and flowers in light-colored wood. The head is bent back from the neck and terminates in a scroll. The finger board is inlaid with ivory and pearl and has no frets. The instrument is strung with eight gut strings tuned in pairs.

A small Italian instrument with a lute-shaped body is 95285. The neck is long and slender, with a rounded back and nine gut frets. It has three strings of gut.

An instrument which forms a connecting link between the lute and mandolin was called by several slightly different names, including " pandora." The shape of this instrument is like a lute, but it has strings of wire instead of gut. Similar to this is the "mandore" of the Moors (95737, pl. 41a). Another Moorish instrument was the gimbrede, characterized by tuning pegs crossing like an X, and having a parchment belly over an elongated body. Two tuning pegs are seen on 95742 (pl. 42a) and three are on 95747 (pl. 42c), which is painted in colors. These instruments were sounded by a plectrum consisting of a narrow strip of bone.

The Russian pandora is a very old instrument, entirely out of use at the present time. An excellent example of this instrument, from Little Russia, is 96463. There are no frets on the finger board and it was played with a quill. The body is oval, with shallow rounded back and flat belly. The six openings of the sound hole are like the petals of a flower. The instrument has 4 stopped brass strings on the finger board and 14 open brass strings across the body. No. 95259 (pl. 34b) has a full rounded back built up of narrow thin staves of ivory with an ebony purfling between, except the staves next the belly, which are of tortoise shell. The belly is of thin unvarnished pine, having a circular sound hole bordered with black, inlaid with pearl, and set with colored stones. On the end of the head is a square ivory plate with a topaz in the center. It is strung with eight overspun strings tuned in pairs and one steel string.

A small Egyptian tanboura is 95244. An Italian pandora of the fifteenth and sixteenth centuries (95251) has 14 wire strings, the lowest of which is overspun. From this instrument the modern mandolin was developed toward the end of the eighteenth century. It has a deeper convexity of back than the lute and was always played with a plectrum.

Several types of mandolin arose in Italy, but the principal types were known as the Neapolitan and Milanese or Lombardy. The former had four pairs of strings tuned in fifths like a violin, and the latter had five or sometimes six pairs of strings with a variable tuning. The largest number of frets on either instrument was 17, and the strings were plucked with a plectrum of tortoiseshell, whalebone, horn, or ostrich quill. An Italian mandolin of the Milanese type (95260) has 6 pairs of strings and 12 frets, and an American mandolin of the Neapolitan type (72880, pl. 35a) has 4 pairs of strings and 13 frets. Special attention is directed to an old Italian mandolin (95261, pl. 34d) labeled " Vendelio Venere of Padua, 1607." The circular sound hole has a black border inlaid with carved ivory and pearl, and the sound hole is filled with a carved open rosette. The head terminates in a carved ivory dog's head. It is strung with one overspun string and eight steel wires tuned in pairs.

A beautiful old Italian instrument is 95307 (pl. 35c), its head terminating in a small human head. The instrument has three gut strings and is labeled " Giuseppe Mascatto Da Rorere Feelt, 1637."

An Egyptian mandolin (95240) has no frets and the strings of gut are plucked with a horn plectrum. The outer edge of the body is inlaid with colored wood, ivory, and mother-of-pearl. No 95910 is a mandolin from Peru, and 15250 comes from Guatemala. The back of the latter instrument is of gourd, and it has five gut strings and five frets that are also of gut. It was received by the Museum in 1874.

A primitive two-stringed guitar from the Poonocks in Alaska is 15615. The body is made of a block of wood, and the belly of thin wood is fastened to the body with pegs.

A peculiar instrument of music is the " alligator guitar " from Burma (95492). The body is carved from a block of wood in the form of a crocodile hollowed and left open. It is strung with three strings, one of copper and two of silk, starting from a staple near the neck of the animal, passing over seven blocks of wood on its back, which act as frets, and fastened to tuning pegs in the tail. Similar to this is 94923, from the Malay of Singapore. It is called an alligator guitar, though the exact form of the animal is left to the imagination.

Among the stringed instruments exhibited with the guitars will be found a Malay instrument (94921), its strings picked by the fingers. It was used at marriage feasts and festivals. Another specimen, from Singapore (94920), was used on similar occasions and is decorated with inlays of stars, crescents, and bands of mother of pearl. These have double bands of rattan around the necks as frets. A Syrian instrument (95144, pl. 35d) is inlaid with triangles of mother of pearl, and ornamented with coins, charms, etc., hung from the head. Nos. 72974 and 72972 are Russian, the latter painted black and both having the finger board inlaid with bone, pearl, and brass.

Two interesting instruments from northern Africa are made from tortoise shells, the plastrum removed and a belly of parchment stretched across and glued to the back. One of these (94654) is decorated with a painting of a bird in colors, and on the neck with an arabesque design in blue outlined with white on a green ground. The bridge and strings are missing. No. 95741 (pl. 42b) has two strings passing over an oval-shaped bridge. Another Moorish instrument (93518) has a body carved from a block of wood in a shape suggesting that of an elongated spoon. It has two strings, and the entire instrument is painted in Moorish designs in six bright colors on a deep red ground. It is played with a quill split in two. A second example from Morocco (95748) has half a gourd shell as its body. The belly is of rawhide, the edges gathered together with a rawhide thong and laced with a thong across the back. Special attention is directed to the manner in which this instrument is strung and tuned. The three gut strings are attached at one end to leather thongs tied around the neck of the instrument, and are tuned by slipping these thongs up and down the neck. Stuck in the upper end of the neck is a feather-shaped ornament of wrought iron, its edges pierced with small holes in which are hung rings of wire.

A curious instrument from Singapore is 95068. It has a boat-shaped body, the long projecting prow forming the neck. This was hollowed out and a back of thin wood lashed to it with a complicated lashing of split rattan. It is strung with two brass wires.

From Mozambique, Africa, we have 94662, which has two strings, one passing over frets and the other along the side of the bar. The instrument has a gourd resonator.

An interesting native instrument from Kongo, Africa, is 174756. It has a spoon-shaped body and a belly of thin skin fastened with wooden pegs, while the cavity of the neck is covered with a thin board of light-colored wood. It has three strings of vegetable fiber. The bridge is missing.

One of the most interesting primitive instruments in this class is 95749, from Tangiers, having a trough-shaped body made from a block of wood. The belly is rawhide stretched over the body, sides, and edges, and laced across the back with a rawhide thong. It has three gut strings, fastened at one end to three prongs and at the other to leather thongs wound and tied around the neck. Transverse holes are made in the neck, from which are hung shells, strings of cloves, beads of all kinds, and two bags made of silk patchwork. From the end of the neck projects a wrought-iron feather with brass rings along the sides. With the instrument are two porcupine quills, which were probably used as plectra. The belly is made taut by forcing small bits of wood between the lacing and the body.

The evolution of the guitar will now be traced. It differs from the mandolin and kindred instruments in having a flat back, as well as in its general outline. The cither is probably the earliest instrument that resembles the modern guitar. A Venetian cither of the year 1760 is exhibited (95264). It has a narrow guitar-shaped body and the sound hole is filled with an inverted cone of openwork called the "sunken rose." This was made of parchment and considered highly decorative in the eighteenth century. The finger board and head of this instrument are ornamented with plates of engraved ivory and the back of the neck is inlaid with ivory and black diamonds. There are 14 fixed frets, 11 of metal on the finger

board and 3 of ebony on the body of the instrument. It is strung
with steel wires. For comparison a Spanish cither is shown (95566,
pl. 36b). This is little used in Spain at the present time, and a
model was made for the Museum in 1893. The chitarra battente
(95048) is described by Mr. Hawley as " a cross between the guitar,
lute, mandolin, and zither. It has the rounded back made up of
longitudinal strips like the lute, the vertical incurving sides and
waist of the guitar, the flat belly sloping back from the bridge like
the mandolin, and is wire strung like the zither." The specimen
exhibited is strung with 10 steel wires, 4 of which are overspun.
Another Italian specimen of this instrument is 95262 (pl. 35b),
which is larger and is ornamented with a fancy plate of tortoise
shell. The sound hole is filled with carved openwork, known as the
"sunken rose."

Many variants of the guitar were in use before the present form
became established. Engel states that " during the latter half of the
eighteenth century lyre-shaped guitars were fashionable among the
ladies of Paris, because playing on them was thought to be graceful,
but as they were inconvenient to hold and presented no real advantage over other forms of the guitar they were gradually abandoned."
An example of a lyre-shaped guitar is 95326 (pl. 41b). During the
nineteenth century a lute-shaped guitar was in use, the exhibited
specimen being 95263 (pl. 36d), inlaid with mother-of-pearl and
having a finger board of tortoise shell. The harp lute was invented
in England by Light, about the beginning of the nineteenth century.
It has a double neck, the posts connected at the top by a curved crossbar (95323).

The guitar, as it is known to-day, has incurving, graceful sides
suggesting the time when the instrument was either bowed or
plucked, it is usually strung with 6 strings—3 of catgut and 3 of silk
wound with silver wire. Its compass is between 3 and 4 octaves upward from the second E below middle C. Probably its greatest
popularity has been in Spain, but it has had periods of popularity
in France and England.

The oldest guitar exhibited is 93645, a Russian model made in
Berlin in 1808. The back and sides are of maple, the belly of pine
or spruce, the neck and head of walnut and the finger board of ebony
with 20 fixed frets. It is tuned and strung like the modern guitar.
An interesting and valuable specimen from England is 95325 (pl.
36a) which has a pear-shaped body, the sound hole of which is fitted
with an openwork rosette of gilt metal. The design represents the
sun surrounded by musical instruments. The finger board is plated
with tortoise shell. It has " Preston's screw-tuning device," the
screws tuned with a small socket key like a watch key which is

shown with the instrument. Other old English instruments are 96475 (pl. 36e) and 324845.

An interesting guitar (326752, pl. 36c) has the name "Jerome" stamped on both screw heads. It is the gift of Miss Le C. Gaillard.

Several exhibited guitars were made in America, one being a Spanish model (55690). It has horizontal tuning pegs with a worm wheel moved by vertical screws. Three instruments made in America show slight differences except in the woods (55689, 55691, and 55692).

Three octave guitars are shown. An American instrument (219989) is much smaller than the ordinary guitar and both back and belly are slightly arched. It is wire strung and tuned like a mandolin. An octave guitar (75608) is from the Portuguese on the Madeira Islands and has gut strings. It is a favorite instrument among the natives, who frequently make the body in the form of a fish, the surface being carved to represent scales. No. 95909 is an octave guitar from Peru.

The collection contains a large guitar (216504), which was used in a band of fine instruments in Manila, P. I. Still larger is 216507, whose strings have a vibrating length of 24 inches.

The name "guitar" is applied to several instruments that lack the characteristics of the foregoing. The Siamese guitar (27310) has a body that is almost circular with vertical sides and is strung with the silk strings that seem a contribution of China and neighboring countries to the development of stringed instruments. A Chinese guitar with an octagonal body is 54126. Like the preceding instrument it has four silk strings tuned in pairs. The interval between the pairs of strings is said to be a fifth. The strings pass over a bridge and 13 high ivory frets. The "balloon guitars," 96570 and 130449 (pl. 44c), are the style of instrument used in northern China and have four silk strings. A Japanese balloon guitar (94643) resembles a lute more than a guitar. A wide leather band glued across the belly is decorated with a raised sun and crescent in ivory. A Chinese banjo (54020, pl. 44f), with three silk strings, has both the belly and back of snake skin, stretched over the body, forced into a groove and glued in place.

Two balalaika or triangular guitars from Alaska are 72553 and 73021. The former comes from Lesnoi Island, collected by W. J. Fisher. It has five gut frets and three strings of the same material. The latter comes from the Commander Islands and is doubtless of Russian origin. It is made of wood and fastened together with wooden pins. Near this is shown a Chilcat guitar with balloon-shaped body, flat back and belly (45971). The head has a nail placed vertically for a tuning peg. One string of twisted sinew passes over a bridge and also over a smaller bridge which acts as a nut.

An Italian instrument with a balloon-shaped body and vertical sides is No. 95249. The head is shaped like half a spearhead, terminating in a scroll.

The banjo is a modern instrument with five to nine strings and occupies a place midway between the guitar and zither. It is commonly associated with the negro and his plantation melodies and can not claim an exalted musical value. An interesting peculiarity of the banjo is the placing of the melody string (which is highest in pitch) outside of and next to the lowest strings, and attaching it to a tuning peg half way up the neck of the instrument. This melody string is played by the right thumb. The strings are stopped by the left hand and plucked or struck with the right, the instrument being played the same as a guitar.

An interesting series of three banjos, showing the development of the instrument, was presented by William Boucher, jr., of Baltimore, a maker of banjos and inventor of certain improvements. A banjo with two heads (94764, pl. 37c) was labeled "First screw-head banjo. Style of 1845." The improvements made during 1846 are shown on 94765, which has only one head. A banjo made in 1847 has 14 screw bolts with square nuts turned with a wrench (94766). A fine instrument, made in 1860 by Fred Mather, was presented by his estate (207888, pl. 37e). The tightening hoop is of metal, silver plated, drawn down by 20 screw bolts with hooped heads; these bolts pass through brackets and are fitted with nuts having square heads. A socket key that fits these nuts accompanies the instrument. No. 55720, obtained in 1882, has 24 brackets and screw bolts. Another banjo of the same year is 55718 (pl. 37d). A "parlor or ladies' banjo" is 55721 (pl. 37a), and an example of the "piccolo or octave banjo" is exhibited as 55723 (pl. 37b).

A Chinese three-stringed banjo (52020) is in the collection. A similar instrument is 54021. No. 95567 is a "student's instrument," obtained in Spain by Dr. Walter Hough. It is pear shaped, with brass jingles set in the hoop. The belly is of goatskin, fastened in place with a flat gilded hoop of wood nailed to the sides.

The zither is a modern member of the great family of stringed instruments plucked with a plectrum. It may be called the national instrument of Bavaria and Tyrol, for it is played by all classes and no inn is without one. It consists of a flat box, which is placed on a table. Over this box run a variable number of strings, some of which are "open" and used in playing the accompaniment, while others are "stopped" by pressing them against frets. A typical instrument has 5 metal strings over the frets and 27 to 40 strings of various sorts which are not fretted. A characteristic of the instrument is the plectrum, which is usually of metal, and may be described as an open ring with a sharp spur. It is worn on the thumb and used on the accompaniment strings, which are nearest the player, while the open strings are plucked by the fingers.

An Italian zither (95238) has 33 strings. Two American concert zithers are 55688, received by the Museum in 1882, and 93646 (pl. 47a), with 5 stopped and 27 open strings, was received in 1887 as a gift from Rudolph Heinrichs.

The psaltery, an important member of this class of instruments, is considered on page 91.

The koto is the national instrument of Japan and is characterized by its long, narrow, sounding board. While the koto of the present day is the result of a long period of development, the form of the instrument has always been the same. According to Piggott "the koto is fantastically supposed to be a dragon, symbolical of all that is noble and precious, lying on the seashore holding such sweet converse with the waves that the angels come to sit and listen by his side." Thus the upper surface of the instrument is called the dragon's back and the under surface his belly. The upper part of the side is a seashore, the long bridge at the right end is the dragon's horn, and the projection is his forked tongue. The long bridge at the left end is the horn of cloud or the angel's seat and the projection is the dragon's tail.

The numerous forms of the instrument are divided by Piggott into three groups:

First, those with one or more strings tuned in unison or to a fifth attached to tuning pegs and played with a "tsumé" [plectrum], the notes being produced by stopping; secondly, those with a fixed bridge at each end with many strings tuned in different ways but without tuning pegs, the strings being permanently stretched and the notes produced by stopping as before, the tsumé not being used in general; thirdly, those with a movable bridge or loose fret for each string.

The material of koto strings is tightly twisted silk soaked in wax, the strings frequently varying in thickness and in heaviness of waxen coating. The length of the instrument is a little more than 6 feet; it is laid on the ground and the player squats near the upper end of it. Two ivory plectra are used, one (a section of a cylinder) being held between the thumb and first finger of the right hand and the other (a heavy cylinder 2½ inches long) being worn on the second finger of the left hand.

The one-stringed koto is said to have been invented in the Engí era, A. D. 901. Tradition states that it was invented by an exiled nobleman to chase away his melancholy, his original instrument being a string stretched across his hat. A one-stringed koto

(96840, pl. 30*f*) has no sound box, the strings being stretched on a curved board which is deeply grooved on the underside with five grooves cut by a gouge. The string passes through an ivory eyelet in the body, thence through a small hole in a rounded stick of hard redwood, and thence to a vertical tuning peg. It is ornamented with 12 small figures of birds (1 missing) and 1 small disk of ivory, probably to indicate where the string should be stopped, and a sunken panel of tortoise shell framed in redwood.

A two-stringed koto (95719) has a sound box, open at the end, and rests on a stand ornamented with purple silken cords like those on the instrument. The strings are stretched between bridges, and on the body of the instrument are six small figures of birds in low relief, possibly to show where the strings should be stopped.

The foregoing examples of the koto belong to the first class of instrument. No specimen of the second class is exhibited. The third class of koto is distinguished by its greater number of strings and its movable bridges. The sounding board is hollowed out inside and the strings are stretched between permanent bridges or nuts at each end of the instrument, all the strings being the same size and length. The difference in pitch is made by small movable bridges, one for each string, which raises them to a height of at least 2 inches above the sounding board; thus each string produces only one tone. The position of these bridges is sometimes changed rapidly during a performance. Besides this, the fingers of the performer's left hand are used to press a certain one of the strings, thus raising the pitch one or two semitones, as may be desired. The plucking of the strings is done with the "tsumé" already described. Long ago a Japanese named Yatsuhashi devoted much study to making improvements in the koto, insisting chiefly upon the use of hard "kiri" wood, thoroughly seasoned, for the sounding board. He called his earliest attempts the "autumn mist" and the "murmuring of the pines" koto and as a result of his labors the modern forms of the instrument were developed. One of these is used by professionals, and its beauty consists in the beautiful graining of the natural wood; the other is known by the name of his pupil, Ikuta, and is elaborately decorated. It is used chiefly by lady amateurs.

Three specimens of the Ikuta-Koto are exhibited. The body of 94958 is of thin kiri wood and rests on four low feet. It is strung with 13 silk strings, each having an adjustable, inverted Y-shaped bridge and two fixed bridges at the ends of the belly. No. 95718 has a flat back of kiri wood and the belly is formed of nine joints of Satsuma bamboo, split lengthwise, and pressed to form about a third of a cylinder. It has 13 silk strings colored green, pink, white, and black. The bridge is gold lacquered with applied designs in light-colored bamboo and brocade silk. Special attention is directed to 93198 (pl. 33d), a magnificent Ikuta-Koto from Tokyo which was exhibited at the Centennial Exhibition in 1876. The fixed bridges near each end are 59¼ inches apart and the 13 silk strings are passed over movable bridges. The instrument is richly decorated with carved ebony and ivory, and on its sides are 24 sandalwood medallions illustrating the classical Japanese story of the 24 obedient children.

Similar to the koto in some respects are two Korean instruments, 93569 and 95207. These are placed on the floor when played and picked with a small rod of bamboo the size of a lead pencil. It will be noted that the outer string on each side does not pass over the bridge, but has an adjustable bridge of its own.

A large group of stringed instruments in India are designated as "vina," "vin," or "bin." The characteristics of this group are a resonator (frequently of gourd), a long finger board, and seven strings, only four of which pass over the finger board, the others being attached to tuning pegs halfway up the neck of the instrument and played as open strings. Some forms of the vina have frets, others have none; some varieties of the instrument are played with a plectrum of wood, steel, or iron, and others are always struck with the finger tips, these variations indicating the wide modifications of the instrument. According to Day, the principal stringed instruments in India (various forms of vina) "still remain just as they are described in the ancient books, even down to the very details of the carving with which they are adorned, so conservative are the people [in matters] connected with the art they hold to be so sacred." Many of the vina have a peacock carved on some part of the instrument. According to Engel this is explained as follows: "Saraswati, the consort of Brahma, * * * is the goddess of music as well as of speech; to her is attributed the invention of the systematic arrangement of the sounds into a musical scale. She is represented seated on a peacock and playing on a stringed instrument of the lute kind." Every vina has its nut carved with an elephant at one end and a peacock at the other. These represent the first and last notes of their musical scale, the different notes of which are represented by animals.

The three principal types of this group are the vina, having a fretted finger board and gourd or wooden resonator; the tambura, which has no frets and a gourd or wooden resonator; and the setar, which resembles the tambura, but has frets on the finger board. To these may be added the small setar played by ladies as a drawing-room instruments. The names of these instruments are spelled in various ways, the form given being that used by Doctor Tagore. Examples of the three types will be designated and the general shape of the instrument will identify other specimens. It is customary to designate instruments with differences from these types as "loud toned," "beautiful toned," or "colorful" vinas.

Vinas with fretted finger board, designated as the first type, are different in northern and southern India. The vina used in northern India (92681, pl. 38b) has two gourd bodies attached by short wooden posts to a horizontal, straight, hollow bar of wood. In the bottom of each gourd is a round opening, and at the lower end of the bar or neck is a carved representation of a peacock. The instrument has seven strings, two of which are attached to tuning pegs at the side of the neck. It has 16 adjustable frets tied to the neck with gut strings and giving semitone intervals. The bridge is a low block of bone or ivory and the nut is similar material having the outline of an elephant's head at one end and that of a peacock at the other. Four of the strings are steel and three are of brass. When in use the gourd with the tuning pegs rests on the left shoulder of the player and the other gourd rests on his right knee. The strings are stopped with the left hand and struck with the right hand, the two first fingers of which are armed with wire plectra. This instrument is difficult to play, but its sound in the hands of a skillful performer is said to resemble that of a piano, but with greater delicacy.

The vina used in southern India has a pear-shaped resonator carved from wood, instead of a gourd. The opening below the strings is covered with tightly stretched parchment. Sometimes a globular wooden resonator is added near the upper end of the finger board. The number of strings is the same as in the vina with the two resonators, but the system of tuning is much simpler. The instrument is taught in the schools in many places and is a favorite with amateurs of the higher classes. It is always played with the finger nails. The strings are made by a process kept secret in a particular caste.

The second class of vina, known as tumbara, is represented by 54069 (pl. 38a). Comparison with the other vina will show that it lacks frets on the finger board and that the tuning pegs are placed differently, those of the first and second strings being placed on opposite sides; it also differs in having no short strings attached half way up the neck. The bridge (absent in the specimen) is movable and has no metal in its fittings. The body of this instrument is painted green and powdered with gilt stenciled flowers, the belly and neck are covered with cloth of silver. It is always held upright when played, the body resting on the ground. The tone is slightly buzzing, and to produce this effect bits of quill or silk are placed between the bridge and strings. It is used only for accompaniments.

The third class of vina, known as the "setar," is perhaps the commonest of all the stringed instruments of India and is fairly easy to learn. It has a peculiar, somewhat jangling tone, the tender charm and coloring of the vina being entirely lacking. It will be noted that the setar has frets on the finger board, though in other respects it resembles the tumbara. The frets are of brass or silver, tied to the finger board, an arrangement which permits their being shifted so as to produce the intervals of any desired scale. The body is usually of gourd, with a belly of thin wood pierced with a certain number of sound holes. The number of strings varies from three to seven. It is played by means of a plectrum of wire on the forefinger, the thumb being usually pressed firmly upon the edge of the instrument. No. 92680 is an example of the "setar."

Two specimens of the kinnari vina are 92683 (pl. 39b) and 54071. The body of the former consists of half the shell of an ostrich egg, which is the usual material. The body of the latter is the same size and shape, but is of silver, and the neck and head are covered with silver cloth. A similar instrument, called a sauktika vina (92686, pl. 39a) has, as its body a pearly shell, the *Nautilus pompilus*. A vina which is said to be bowed as well as picked is 92692. The body and neck are made of a block of wood, the sides deep and almost vertical. It has six gut strings and seven sympathetic wires which pass through holes in the bridge and are tuned by pegs set in the side of the instrument.

Other interesting vinas are 92690, which has two fretted finger boards, and 92684, which has a body made of a double gourd and a belly of thin wood. A peculiar little setar with fluted sides is 92682. The first and second strings are of brass tuned in unison, and the third of steel tuned a fourth higher. No. 92687 is a vina with body made of the stem end of a gourd and a head of parchment glued to the body. This is a modern instrument formed from the vina of southern India and the setar.

A particularly interesting vina is 92699, described by Mr. Hawley as follows:

The body is a nearly entire gourd held by a trumpet-shaped piece of wood which is surmounted by a small carved peacock. The neck is of bamboo and projects horizontally from the tail of the peacock. The nut is made of thin wood, blackened, tied with a cord and cemented with black wax. The bridge is of bone and rests on the turned-up tail of the peacock.

A large vina (92685, pl. 39d), received from the Rajah of Tagore in 1883, has half a gourd as its body. It owes its name to the flat gourd, supposed to resemble the back of a tortoise (kach hapa). The neck is large, half round, and hollowed, the cavity covered with a finger board that has down its middle a sunken panel 3 inches wide in which are seven sympathetic strings tuned by pegs in the side of the neck. Sixteen iron frets span the sympathetic strings. The tuning of the melody strings is accomplished by means of five tuning pegs at the end and two on the side of the neck.

An instrument called a rudra vina (92691, pl. 39c) as a resonator carved from a block of wood, gourd shaped, but ribbed or fluted. The belly of parchment is glued in place. This form of vina is a favorite in Persia and the northern provinces of India.

INSTRUMENTS WITH OPEN STRINGS, HAMMERED

The principal representative of this group is the dulcimer. Consideration is here given to the psaltery, however, because of a resemblance between the psaltery and dulcimer, and because both were ancestors of the keyboard group. The psaltery, as will be noted, was a predecessor of the spinet, and the dulcimer led naturally to the hammerclavier, or pianoforte.

The psaltery is an instrument of great antiquity. "It is frequently mentioned in the Bible together with the harp, though it seems to have been used less than the latter." The psaltery is also mentioned by Chaucer and the English and French romanticists. The strings of a psaltery are stretched over a sounding board and only a short distance above it. The instruments formerly in use were trapeze shaped; they differ from the dulcimer only in the manner of being played, the strings of the psaltery being picked and those of the dulcimer being struck with hammers.

An excellent example of the psaltery is 95180 (pl. 40c), an Egyptian instrument. It has 72 strings of camel gut, colored black. They are arranged in groups of three, the group being tuned to one pitch, as in the piano. With the instrument is a pair of plectra, each consisting of a metal band and a whalebone pick. No. 95181 is similar except that it has 78 strings. Like the former, it is tuned to the diatonic scale with the Cs and Fs sharped.

A Turkish instrument closely resembling this is 93880. A Finnish psaltery (95691) has its top projecting in the form of a scroll.

The Chinese orchestral instruments collected by John B. Henderson have already been mentioned. Among these is a Chinese psaltery (94847) which is 78 inches long and has 25 silk strings tuned in pairs. Under each string is a movable bridge like that of a koto. Another Chinese psaltery (54024, pl. 33a) is shorter, has one fixed bridge, and is strung with 16 brass wires of graduated lengths. It was received in 1876 as a gift from the Chinese Imperial Centennial Committee. With this is pictured a Korean stringed instrument (95207, pl. 33b) with 6 strings, 3 of which pass over fixed frets, while the other 3 have each a movable bridge like that of a koto.

A curious instrument (95726), probably from Madagascar, was collected in 1893. It consists of a section of bamboo with seven strings cut from the cuticle and left attached to the bamboo at both ends. Small pieces of wood are crowded between the strings and the body to lift up the strings, each bit of wood being like a bridge. A braided hoop of split rattan is placed around the bamboo over the ends of the strings to prevent their further expansion.

An instrument that attracts the attention is 95121, from Celebes Island. It consists of a body made of a section of bamboo with a resonator made of a palm leaf. Eighteen brass wires are attached to tuning pegs with arrow-shaped heads, which are arranged in two rows around the bamboo body. By their structure the two last-named are classified as psalteries.

The dulcimer resembles the psaltery so closely in its form that one description might serve for both instruments, but the manner of playing is entirely different. The psaltery, as already indicated, is picked with a plectrum and the dulcimer is struck with hammers, the heads of which are covered with hard leather on one side and with soft leather on the other side. The player holds one in each hand and uses them as desired to produce certain effects.

The oldest dulcimer in the collection is 95290 (pl. 40b), made in 1600. It is an Italian instrument, painted with cupids and wreaths in colors that are now dim and faded. It has a compass of 33 tones. An Italian dulcimer of the eighteenth century (94868) has 80 brass wires arranged in groups of four, one of which is of doubled and twisted wire. Probably the three single wires of each group were tuned in unison and the twisted wires an octave below. A dulcimer from Calcutta is of a sort sometimes called the "hundred-string vina" on account of the large number of wires. This specimen (92693) is supposed to be tuned in the diatonic scale from —3G to G.

Four Chinese dulcimers are exhibited. The most ornate is 96493 (pl. 40a) with its body of lacquered blackwood, shaped in many curves. It has two circular sound holes filled with openwork ivory carvings. There are fixed bridges at each end and two rows of seven bridges with an open space between each row. It is strung with 14 groups of brass wires, 10 of which are doubled and twisted, and it is played with two slender elastic strips of bamboo, their heads projecting from one side of the handle. Two circular sound holes filled with openwork alabaster plates distinguish 125897. It has two bridges, the wires passing alternately through holes in one bridge and over the other. It is played with two wooden hammers of a peculiar shape. The tuning key is in a small drawer in the body of the instrument. Other Chinese dulcimers are 54025 and 96642.

An American dulcimer made about the year 1875 is 94872. It has 44 wires tuned in pairs. With it are two hammers having bone handles, a flat steel spring shaft and stuffed buckskin heads. An

Italian dulcimer decorated with a painting is 95318. With this group is exhibited an Italian "tuning instrument" (95311), strung with seven steel wires.

INSTRUMENTS WITH STRINGS, BOWED

The stringed instruments thus far considered have had their strings set in vibration by plucking or striking. Sometimes this was done with the fingers and sometimes with a plectrum or a rod, either fastened to the fingers or held in the hand.

We are now to observe a series of instruments whose strings are set in vibration by friction. To this series belong the familiar instruments of the violin family. The implement with which the strings are frictioned is called a bow, and probably originated in a somewhat rough plectrum. The Hindu ascribe the invention of the bow to Ravanon, a mighty king of Ceylon who lived about 5,000 years ago and invented an instrument called a "ravanastron." It seems probable, however, that so simple a device may have originated in more than one place. The bows used by ancient and primitive peoples are widely varied and strung with vegetable fiber as well as hair. The development of the present violin bow from these beginnings is too extended a study for detailed description. As will be seen, the bow was not of European origin, but was introduced into Europe chiefly through northern Africa.

It will be noted that some stringed instruments were both plucked and bowed, the latter method of vibrating the strings gradually taking the place of the former method. Probably the raised bridge was a determining factor between the guitar fiddle and the ancestors of the tenor viol.

The term "fiddle" is commonly applied to all bowed instruments irrespective of their outline, and the term "violin" is reserved for designating the instrument known by that name at the present time.

Bowed stringed instruments will be considered under three classes, having as their representative types the crwth, rebec, and viol. Each of these types contributed to the development of the modern violin and related instruments.

The "crwth" was the ancient national instrument of Wales, but has now passed into oblivion. In England the name was changed to "crowd," and a carving of the instrument appears on one of the choir seats at Worcester Cathedral, dated 1397. The Welsh word designates also a scooped-out, bulging article of wood, and "crwth halen" means a salt box. This implies that the instrument once had a rounded back, like a lyre, but in the latter part of the eighteenth century it had a flat back. An excellent copy of the crwth of that period is exhibited (96478, pl. 41*d*). It is oblong in shape, with two oblong openings which enable the player to stop the strings. The body is scooped out of a single block of wood and the belly is glued in place. The bridge is remarkably shallow and is placed in a somewhat oblique direction with one foot passing through one of the circular sound holes and resting on the back of the instrument. It has 6 catgut strings, 4 of which rest on the bridge and were played with a bow; the other 2 run beside the bridge and were twanged with the left thumb or else used as drones. One of these was tuned G below middle C and the other an octave higher. The usual tuning of the four catgut strings was middle C and its octave and the D above middle C with its octave. The top of the bridge is so flat that it is almost impossible to draw the bow across a single string, and it seems probable that the strings were sounded in pairs, as they are tuned in octaves.

The strings are passed through small holes at the top of the neck and fastened at the back of the head to tuning pins that project through the head and are turned at the front of the instrument. This contrivance is very common on the instruments of the Arabs, Persians, and Hindus, and the bridge with one foot through the sound hole is a characteristic of the three-stringed fiddle, a variety of the " rebab." Furthermore, the crwth bears a striking resemblance to the oriental lyre (pl. 41*c*) which was used in Egypt, Greece, and other countries before the Christian era, the only noteworthy difference being the addition of the finger board in the crwth.

Rebab is a generic term for bowed instruments in Moslem countries. The word is said to have been derived from the Persian "revave," meaning "sorrowful toned." It appears that originally the rebab had only one or two strings. Another instrument of this class (the " kamanja ") appears to have had two or three strings. From Persia these instruments found their way into northern Africa, thence to Spain, central Europe, and England. The rebab resembled a mandolin in appearance and was called by many, slightly different names. The " rebec " of western Europe in the Middle Ages was identical with the German geige. The player either rested the larger end of the instrument lightly against his breast or held it like a violin. In either position it was played with a bow. A flattening of the back of the instrument and a slight changing of the outline marked the gradual evolution of the violin group of stringed instruments. When these came into general use the rebec and geige disappeared. The third class, represented by the vial, is considered on page 99.

Having outlined the development of bowed stringed instruments in Persia, the Orient, and Europe, we will note exhibited specimens which illustrate this development. First, a rebab from Morocco

(95738, pl. 42e) has two strings that can not be stopped. The bow is a bent-wood stick covered with red and white flannel, the horsehair tied at each end. The lower half of the belly is of parchment glued to the body. Similar in construction, but unfinished, is 95739. The parchment belly has been glued on, and lacings that held it while the glue dried are still in place. On the finished instrument the edges of the parchment have been cut away. A rebab from Java (95670, pl. 42d) has a pear-shaped body, rounded back, and vertical sides. It has two strings. From Egypt we have two specimens of the rebab el Mooghun'nee. The older specimen is 56195, which was acquired in 1876. The other specimen is 95138, acquired in 1891. Each instrument has a body consisting of a four-sided frame of wood with belly of rawhide or parchment, the back of the frame being left open. The strings are of horsehair and are not twisted. No. 95693 is a copy of the " fiddle and bow " used by the Bedouins and called by them " rebabeh." As an interesting comparison, we note two Italian ribeca (95309 and 95310, pl. 41e), which have three strings tuned in fifths and two rude F-shaped sound holes without a notch in the middle. A modern Greek lyra made on the old lines is 203721. The body, neck, and head are made from a block of oak, the body being excavated. The belly is of pine, about one-fourth inch in thickness, nailed to the body and having two D-shaped sound holes below the bridge. The construction of the bow is interesting. The horsehair is fastened to a rag, which is tied to the frog at the end of the bow, and the tension of the hair is governed by crowding the hand of the player between the rag and the stick. An instrument from the Celebes Islands is No. 95120. The pearshaped body is carved from a block of wood, and the eyes and mouth of a mask carved on the back of the instrument serve as sound holes. It is strung with two brass wires and played with a bow. Another native fiddle from Africa is 151295, used by all the tribes of Angola. It has three strings of vegetable fiber, two of which are single ply, the third two ply. Two fiddles from Tiflis in Russia are entirely different in shape. A bulbous body made of 16 thin bent staves characterizes 72975. The belly is of bladder, and it has three strings, two of brass and one of steel wire. The other instrument from the Caucasus is 72976, which has a coffin-shaped body, made from a block of wood. It has four gut strings and four sympathetic brass wire strings. In the tuning of these strings the highest are at the left, an Arab custom which is the reverse of the European tuning.

The second type of stringed, bowed instrument used in Moslem countries was the " kamanja," a specimen of which is shown as 96480 (pl. 42f). It has a balloon-shaped body made from a block of wood, and three strings that start from the ends of the tuning pegs. The bridge is something like a violin bridge, with the right foot much longer than the left. It has no sound post. Nos. 95241, 95183, and 95184 are kamanja a' gouz from Cairo, the body of the instrument made of a coconut shell, with belly and bladder glued to the shell. The strings are of horsehair, not twisted. They are passed over a bridge of pitch.

A group of the bowed stringed instruments used in India is shown in plate 43. The chikara and sarinda are pastoral instruments, and the sarangi is a drawing-room instrument with which the sarode (or sharadiga vina) is frequently played. A "peacock fiddle," or may-uri, completes this group. As already indicated, the chikara is an instrument of the common people (92704 pl. 43d). The body, neck, and head are made of one block of wood. Its shape is that of an elongated balloon with sides deeply curved inward at the waist. It has three horsehair strings and four sympathetic strings of wire, graduated in length, which pass through eyelet holes in the finger board to their tuning pegs.

The sarinda is a rude form of the saringa and is known to be an ancient instrument (92703, pl. 43a). Its chief peculiarity is the way in which the parchment belly is put on. This is made to cover only the lower part of the body, leaving the upper half quite open. The upper part of the body is larger than the lower and somewhat like a crescent in outline. The tuning is like that of the chikara and the strings are of gut or silk. The instrument exhibited has three gut strings. It is played with a rude imitation of a European bow.

The sarangi, according to Tagore, "is a very sweet-toned ancient instrument, intended to accompany the female voice. It is generally used in the performances of the Hindustani nautch girls." Two specimens of this instrument are exhibited. The larger of these (54072, pl. 43b) is the type commonly found in the south of India and the Deccan. The resin for the bow is ingeniously placed in the head. It has four gut strings and several sympathetic brass wire strings of graduated lengths. The stick of the bow is covered with maroon velvet. The second specimen of sarangi (96494, pl. 43c) is the type found in upper India and the Punjab. It is more highly decorated than the former and the head is a different shape. "The head is generally carved to represent the neck of a swan, and the body is rounded instead of square; the number of sympathetic strings, too, is often less. The manner of tuning and playing are the same as in the sarangi of the south." The instrument exhibited has three brass wires played with a bow and eight sympathetic strings. The neck is carved in the shape of a bird's head, and the body is decorated with sprigs of roses in green and gold, and gilt borders on a red ground. The bow is a cylindrical stick colored black, the hair in a round bundle tied to the stick with strings.

The sarode (92692), according to Tagore, is "a drawing-room stringed instrument played with a wooden Jawa [plectrum] . . . [It is] mostly used in the upper Provinces. It was formerly used as an outdoor instrument in royal possessions." It is also played with a bow and in this usage it "is used to accompany the sarangi as the tenor or second fiddle."

"Mayuri" is the Hindu name for peacock and is also given to an instrument with a body made of wood, carved to represent a peacock, with head, neck, wings, and feet. It is classified as a fiddle, though the strings were sometimes plucked. Day states that it is rarely seen out of upper India, where it is used chiefly by nautch musicians. The specimen exhibited (92696, pl. 43e) has 5 wire strings and 15 sympathetic wires of graduated lengths. The latter pass through eyelets in the finger board to turning pegs placed in a piece of wood fastened to the left side of the neck. This is played with an ordinary fiddle bow. A modern instrument, classified as a bowed vina, is 92689.

Before proceeding to the third class of bowed string instruments (viols), we will consider a group of fiddles and the curious "marine trumpet" with its single string.

The Chinese have a two-stringed instrument "hu hu" similar to the ravanestrum of India and played with a bow. Its strings are tuned a fifth apart. Three typical instruments of this class are 54027, 54028 (pl. 44d), and 54029, which were obtained in 1876 from the Chinese Imperial Centennial Commission. The last named has a belly of snake skin. Similar to this is 130445 (pl. 44a). The bow used with these instruments is a slender wand of bamboo with a hooked peg driven into the bow near the handle. The bow hair is fastened to the tip and the other end of the hair is looped around the hooked peg. When the instrument is played the bow hair is unhitched from the peg, passed over one string and under the other, and then hitched on the peg again. A Chinese fiddle (96651) is part of the Chinese orchestra obtained at Pekin by John B. Henderson and given to the Museum. It is strung with four silk strings tuned in pairs, a fifth apart. An instrument of this shape but having the body a section of coconut shell is called T'i-ch'in. This is played chiefly by blind men. Two specimens are exhibited—54030 and 54031 (pl. 44b).

Four Siamese fiddles having the body made of the shell of the coconut or similar nut are 54065, 54066, and 96582. The first named is peculiar in that the back of the body has a delicate openwork rosette, representing fruits and flowers, for a sound hole. When played the bow hair is passed between the strings so as to go over one and under the other. The second named has a fancy foot, turned like a spire and more than 10 inches long. The bow is a malacca cane and the fingers are crowded between the hair and stick to act as a frog. A similar instrument with two silk strings is 96582-1, while 96582 (pl. 44g) has three strings of doubled and twisted fiber. The belly of thin skin is laced through holes in its edge to a hoop of twisted split rattan around the lower part of the body.

A Japanese fiddle (93203, pl. 44e) has four silk strings, the two highest tuned in unison. The player holds the instrument upright, turning it to right or left as may be necessary to bring it in contact with the bow, which is long and slender.

Two primitive fiddles are from Singapore; they are played like the Chinese instruments. One of these (94926) has the body of coconut shell pierced with sound holes at the back. The bow is a round bamboo stick, the hair passing through holes in the end. A similar instrument (94927) has two silk strings and a belly of snake skin.

Stringed instruments are not native to the American Indians and occur in only a few tribes where the model has undoubtedly been acquired from the white man. Four fiddles of the Apache Indians are shown. Two of these (213280 and 204655) were obtained by Dr. Walter Hough; 5521b was collected by Dr. E. Palmer near Tucson, Ariz.; and the oldest of the group, which was obtained in 1875, is 21536 (pl. 30h). All these are made from the flower stalk of the yucca except the first named, which is made from an agave stalk. The pith is extracted except at the ends, and the fiddle is strung with one string; in one instance this is sinew and in another it is twisted horsehair. The bow is a short, half-round stick, strung with horsehair tied in place with sinew. This instrument, when played, was held at right angles with the body, the lower end of the instrument pressed against the middle of the player's chest. The right hand stopped the strings and the left hand ran the bow back and forth with a motion like sawing the string. A player with his instrument is shown in Plate 45, which is a copy of an old photograph.

In the Middle Ages there were two musical instruments called "marine trumpet" (tromba marina). One was a wind instrument and the other a stringed instrument played with a bow. The former is of little interest at the present time, but the latter was an important ancestor of the violin family. Three examples are shown, 95280 and 95281, obtained in Italy, and 219418, an American reproduction. It was a long, shallow instrument usually open at the base. The front was flat and the back made with several angles. It had only one string and was characterized by a curious, trembling bridge. This marine trumpet was played by nuns and ecclesiastics and there is no record that it was ever used by sailors. Galpin believes it received its name from Marin, the famous French trumpeter, and Engel expresses the opinion that the name may be " a corruption of tromba mariana, implying a trumpet played in honor of the Virgin Mary." Other authorities hold it was named from a resemblance to a speaking trumpet used on Italian vessels. This is an interesting instance of the uncertainty which surrounds the names of medieval musical instruments. There is no doubt that the instrument was used in musical performances at the convents. The trumpet was considered an important instrument in ensemble music and trumpeters were not allowed in the convents, so the nuns made use of this instrument, whose harmonics resembled the tone of a trumpet. We read that " sometimes the nuns were moved to jubilate upon four marine trumpets accompanied by drums."

The marine trumpet, as already stated, had only one string. This was a very thick gut string, stretched over a peculiar bridge, and played with a bow like a violincello bow, heavily rosined. The harmonics, obtained by touching the string lightly with the finger tips, were very pleasing, but " if the strings were pressed down on the finger board in the ordinary manner the tone was far less melodious than the bray of an ass." The entire weight of the string rested on the right end of the bridge, pressing it firmly against the body of the instrument but the left end of the bridge rested lightly and vibrated against the instrument like an organ reed. Without this bridge the instrument was a bowed monochord, but with the addition of this bridge it became a new and unique instrument. Sometimes it was fitted with two, three, or even four strings and in this form it was undoubtedly an ancestor of the German " geige " whence the viol and violin were derived.

The third class of bowed stringed instruments to be considered is the viol, which shows the adaptation of the bow to an instrument with a guitar-shaped body. The early forms of viol have been already noted. They are not unlike the mandolin, but narrower and longer, and, like all bowed instruments, came into Europe from the Orient, chiefly by way of northern Africa and Spain. The viol appeared in Europe during the sixteenth century and became obsolete with the eighteenth century, and its use was the first step toward the violin of the present day. In the Hardanger violin and the viol (viola) d'amore the ordinary strings are supplemented by sympathetic strings tuned in unison with them. The latter is seldom heard to-day, but the quartet of strings—violin, viola, violincello, and bass—form the foundation on which the modern orchestra is built. A Hardanger violin is shown as 95912.

The viols were furnished with frets like the lute and were studied by the greatest masters of music. Owing to the depth of their sides and the flatness of the back, the sound was soft and slightly reedy or nasal but very penetrating. When the violin was introduced the tone was so much more brilliant than that of the viols that it was considered uncultured and not refined; indeed, Thomas Mace refers to the "scoulding violins" that "be fit to make a man's ears glow and to fill his brains full of friskes."

A "sett" of viols, consisting of six members, ranged downward from the soprano to the double bass. Among them were the viol d'amore, the viol de gamba or knee viol (from the Italian gamba, leg), and the viola braccio, or arm viola. Almost all, if not all, of this group of instruments has sympathetic as well as bowed strings. A viol d'amore (95266, pl. 46*f*) has the head terminating in a carved cupid's head with eyes bandaged. The present collection contains three valuable speciments of viola braccio. Nos. 95324 (pl. 46*g*) and 94865 are German instruments made in 1704 and 1703. The former has six melody strings and seven sympathetic strings tuned either in unison or an octave higher. The latter has two sound holes of the sort called the "flaming sword." Attention is directed to the openwork circular sound holes in the viols illustrated. An Italian instrument (95279) was made by Antonius Gragnani, of Liburni, Italy, in 1780. An old "viola or tenor viol" is 94838, labeled "Johan Georg Hennig, New Kirchen 1738." It has the "flaming sword" sound holes. The original number of strings was probably five, six, or more, but it is now strung and tuned like a viola.

An arci viola de lira from Italy (95265) has a heart-shaped head and nine vertical tuning pegs with heads at the back. It does not coincide with descriptions of types, having some characteristics of different instruments of the period of viols.

The double bass (or bass viol) is the largest stringed instrument played with a bow and is the only one of the viol family now in common use. It has the flat back and slanting shoulders that characterized the old viols, while the four corners, the f-holes, and the belly are like the modern violin group. The double bass originally had only three strings, and some players still prefer the three-stringed instrument on account of its greater sonority. Both three-stringed and four-stringed double basses are now in use and the five-stringed bass is rapidly being introduced at the present time. The double bass is about 6 feet high and the strings are so long that they are tuned in fourths to make the intervals more convenient for the hand. If it be a three-stringed instrument, it is tuned to give upward fourths beginning with A below the bass staff. The additional string in a four-stringed instrument gives the pitch of the second E below the bass staff. The player stands beside the instrument, using a short, heavy bow.

The collection contains a three-stringed double bass (95305) which was made by Tommaso Carcassi, Florence, Italy, in 1760. The bridge is very high.

A four-stringed double bass (72847) is 77¼ inches in height, but is described as "three-quarter size." It was made in Germany. The back is flat and slopes toward the neck. The upper end of the body has the pointed arch form that is characteristic of the viol family. It has four strings of gut, two of which are overspun.

It will readily be noted that the three other members of the violin family do not have the pointed arch form at the top, the outline of the shoulders being like that of a guitar. These three instruments are the violin, having four strings tuned upward in fifths from G below middle C and having a range of more than four octaves; the viola, a little larger than the violin, tuned in fifths beginning one-fifth lower than the violin and having a range of above three octaves; and the violincello, tuned in fifths an octave below the viola, larger than that instrument and played in the reversed position, the player being seated.

The history of famous violin makers is summarized as follows by Mr. Hawley:

To Gaspard di Salo, of Bressica, Italy, is ascribed its invention. He flourished between 1560 and 1610. * * * The elder Amati began business in Cremona, Italy, in 1600. Stradivari and Guarneri both worked in Amati's shop. In 1670 Stradivari began to sign his own name to his work. His best work was done between 1700 and 1725; he died in 1737. The violin, as he left it, has been neither improved nor equaled.

The present collection contains copies of the best models. No. 55638 is a copy of a Gaspard di Salo, made in France. There are very few of his original instruments now in existence; one of them was, however, the favorite instrument of Ole Bull. No. 72846 is a copy of a Stradivarius and 55682 (pl. 46b) of a Guarnerius. Another copy of a Guarnerius (55675) is labeled "Josephus Guarnerius fecit Cremona anno 1720." Josephus was the son of Andreas, the first of that family of violin makers. An interesting old French violin is 55680 (pl. 46e), supposed to have been made by the successor of Francois Salzard, who died in Paris, 1875. A particularly fine specimen is 55677 (pl. 46a), a Stainer model made by Hopf, Germany. No. 55679 is a copy of a Jacobus Stainer made in Italy, labeled "Jacobs Stainer in Absam, 1656." It is said that "of all German makers, the most noted was Jacob Stainer, born 1621, died 1683. He was educated in the workshop of Nicolo Amati, and his violins were characterized by pure tones, though they had small sonority." Another German violin is 55676, the back inlaid with mother-of-pearl, and still another is 55675, also decorated. No. 55681 (pl. 46d) is a copy of a Vuillaume (French) said to have been made in Germany. As representatives of French manufacture we have 96610, made by La Prevotte, Paris, in 1834; and 94844, made by Chanot, of Paris, who made many copies of Stradivarius and Guarnerius violins. A Russian model made in Germany in 1850 is 55678.

The viola has a distinctive, rather sad quality of tone and is seldom used in solos. As examples of the viola we have 94839, made by August Riechers, of Germany, in 1872, and an instrument (55686, pl. 46c) which is a copy of a Stradivarius and was made in France. It is strung with four strings, two of gut and two overspun.

The violoncello had at first only two strings and was used as a fundamental bass in the music of the church. In the fifteenth century it had five strings. The present instrument has a full, rich, and penetrating tone, combined with a wonderful range, making it a splendid solo instrument. Three examples are exhibited, all of them made in Germany. They are 55687, 94840, and 94841, the two last-named forming part of the Morris Steinert collection.

Three small instruments of violin shape are "dancing master's fiddles," or "pocket fiddles," and were formerly carried around by dancing masters. They are 95292 and 95293 from Italy, dated 1700; and 94867, from England, dated 1767. Some of these pocket fiddles had three and some had four strings. Two other small violins are for use in teaching children, 55684 being one-quarter size and 55685 being three-quarter size. Both were made in France and strung and tuned like large violins.

Theodore Thomas said that the invention of the present violin bow by Francois Torte made possible the modern orchestra, with its shadings of tone. This remarkable bow maker was born in Paris in 1747 and died in 1835. Among the many violin bows in the collection are two copies of Torte bows (55703 and 55706), and a copy of a Bausch solo bow (55705).

INSTRUMENTS WITH KEYS

The monochord was the beginning of stringed instruments among cultured nations, as the musical bow was the beginning of stringed instruments among primitive peoples. The first use of the monochord was practical rather than musical. According to Hipkins it was " a pitch-measuring string apparatus, employed, as no doubt the very early organs were, as a pitch carrier or interval measurer." The same authority writes that:

Pythagoras measured a vibrating string stretched between raised bridges on a resonance box, and by shifting those bridges he was enabled to accurately determine the intervals of the Greek diatonic scale. It has been supposed Pythagoras found the monochord in Egypt, where the principle of the stopped string upon a finger board had been known, as the monuments testify, ages before his time, and it may have been known in Babylonia. After Pythagoras the monochord became in Greece * * * and in Europe generally, the canon or rule for the measurement of intervals, and continued to be so employed up to the eleventh century and later of our era.

In medieval times the monochord (*monos*, one; *chorda*, string) consisted of a single string stretched over two bridges which were fixed on an oblong box.

HURDY-GURDY

The earliest stringed instrument fitted with keys was probably the hurdy-gurdy, which in the Middles Ages was almost as popular as the pianoforte of the present day. It should be understood that the hurdy-gurdy of medieval times was in no way related to the street organ which in modern times is called by that name. It has always been associated with rural life, like the bagpipe, but in the first half of the eighteenth century it contributed to the amusement of the French higher classes during the years when mock shepherds and shepherdesses were in vogue. It is also called a vielle. The old Latin name for the hurdy-gurdy was organistrum, and this form of instrument was so large that it took two persons to play it. The instrument was so long that two players laid it across their knees, and one turned the crank while the other touched the keys. A typical instrument had only one melody string.

The hurdy-gurdy is allied to both bowed and keyed instruments, as its strings are frictioned and their vibrating length is affected by keys. The friction is accomplished by a wheel, operated by a crank which the player turns with his right hand. Four of the five strings are drones, and sound continuously unless moved away from the wheel by a simple contrivance. The melody string passes over the body of the instrument, and its vibrating length is changed for each note by the pressing of a key, as a violinist stops a string with his fingers. Sometimes two melody strings are used, the pair being tuned in unison. Thus the instrument played a melody with an accompaniment of drone tones, but could not be used for playing part music. As this form of music was greatly enjoyed by the people, the hurdy-gurdy gradually gave way to instruments on which it could be played.

Three specimens of this curious instrument are exhibited. The finest is a French instrument (94866, pl. 47*d*) with four drone strings stretched over the belly on the left and right of the key box. Partially within the body but rising up through the belly is a wooden wheel, placed on a shaft parallel to the strings, and operated by a crank at the end of the instrument. An Italian hurdy-gurdy with 12 keys is 95256, and a native instrument from Little Russia is 96465 (pl. 47*e*). This has three melody strings and two drones. It is said that "the instrument is usually played by blind beggars at fairs and festivals and as they wander from village to village."

The nyckel harpa of Sweden resembles the hurdy-gurdy in the manner of stopping the strings, but differs in the manner of sounding them, the nyckel harpa being played with a bow. A specimen of this curious instrument (216270) has 21 stopping keys similar to those of a hurdy-gurdy. The instrument is suspended by a ribbon around the player's neck and hangs in such a position that the keys fall downward by their own weight. The player presses them upward to secure the desired tones. The bow is of primitive form and has no frog, the player's finger being crowded between the hair and the string for that purpose.

SOLOPHONE

The solophone (219990, pl. 47c) is a stringed instrument played with a bow and having 20 keys which press down the strings as a violin player would press them with his fingers.

INSTRUMENTS WITH KEYBOARD

CLAVICHORD

As noted, the hurdy-gurdy was a monochord, its melody string set in vibration by a wheel and divided into vibrating sections by the pressure of little keys or plugs. Some ingenious musician introduced a simple leverage by which one end of a little bar was depressed and the other end correspondingly elevated, and the whole development of keyboard instruments became possible. A little wooden upright like the end of a screw driver was put on the end of the key bar that struck the string, giving more force to the contact. The resultant instrument was called a clavichord (clavis, key; chorda, string), and had a keyboard producing the tones of about three octaves. By the use of numerous keys it was possible to secure a rather wide range of tones from a smaller number of strings, the little wooden uprights being placed at a different distance from the end on each key bar, and having diagonal connections so arranged that the operation of one key did not interfere with that of another. The strings were stretched between two fixed bridges and the vibrating length was that portion of the string between the fixed bridge nearest the player and the point at which it was stopped. It was stopped by the key lever. Strips of cloth were wound in and out across the ends of the strings nearest the second, or farther, bridge, acting as dampers to that part of the strings. In the early clavichords one string (or set of strings tuned in unison) could be set in vibration by two or even more keys with tangents at slightly different points on the key bar. These were called "fretted clavichords." The principal developments were marked by the use of one key for each string (such clavichords being called "unfretted"), and by the use of two strings tuned in unison instead of a single string. In the latter instruments the upright at the end of the key bar was broadened so that it struck both strings at the same time. A model of the instrument is 95790.

The clavichord was much more expressive than the harpsichord and was the favorite instrument of John Sebastian Bach. It was carried by Mozart on his musical journeys, and Beethoven also was partial to the instrument.

An interesting old clavichord is 94886, brought from Bohemia in 1791 by Henrietta Decker. It is supposed to have been made in 1741. There are two wires to each note, and the instrument was placed on a table when played. It was collected among the Moravians of Pennvania by John B. Kevinski.

In the course of time a musician saw the key principle used on the clavichord and put a plectrum on the upright at the end of the key lever. When he pressed the key downward the plectrum, forced upward, twanged the string. This was the inception of the spinet, virginal, harpsichord, and similar instruments, which, in method of tone production, were psalteries twanged mechanically by means of a keyboard. The dulcimer was at first a small, flat instrument, placed on a table when played. Later it was made with longer strings set in a rectangular frame with legs at the corners, but the strings were still struck by hammers held in the player's hands. Nevertheless it contributed to the development of the pianoforte, in which hammers were substituted for plectra at the ends of the key bars, vibrating the strings by percussion instead of by plucking, as in the spinet group of instruments. The early forms of the psaltery and dulcimer are considered on page 91.

SPINET AND VIRGINAL

The name "spinet" is applied to a group of keyboard stringed instruments with one string to each note, vibrated by twanging. The name is said to have been derived from the little crow-quill plectrum, somewhat resembling a thorn (Latin spina) with which the strings were sounded. In England the instrument was called a virginal. Neither of these, however, was the original name, for in 1404, in the rules of the Minnesingers, the instrument was called a "clavicymbolum." Various names were given the instrument in various countries, and it was made in oblong, trapeze, and wing shape. There was also an upright spinet called a clavicytherium, which in some instances had gut strings. The early keyboard of the spinet group followed the keyboard of the organs of that day and had keys of such width that the player could compass an octave with his hand. The earlier organ keys were so wide that a player could compass only a fifth. Boxwood seems to have preceded ivory for the lower (natural) keys, while the upper (sharp or flat) keys were of ebony or were stained a dark color. The present arrangement of ivory and ebony keys came into use during the last 30 or 40 years of the eighteenth century. A model of the instrument is 95789.

The first great manufacturer of spinets was Hans Rucker, of Antwerp, who lived about 1579. The work was continued by his son, Andreas, in 1620, and by English makers a century later. The compass of the instrument was three and one-half to five octaves and, as indicated, it had one string to each key. Sometimes a small instrument, tuned an octave higher than the large instrument, was slipped into the frame at one end of the keyboard. This could be taken out and placed on a table so that the performer could play both instruments with more convenience. Elaborate paintings adorn many of the old spinets.

A transverse or wing-shaped spinet (95828, pl. 48) was made by Joseph Mahoon, London, in 1797, and was given to the Museum by H. A. and F. H. Vinton, of Bedford Village, N. Y. It has one wire to each key, picked by jacks with quill points.

A fine Italian virginal (95828, pl. 49) was made by Joannes Baptista Bonomen in 1602. The original color of the case was blue green. On the inside of the cover may still be seen the paintings of old musical instruments and a scene representing the sports and pastimes of the seventeenth century.

A virginal of the seventeenth century (95236), collected in Florence by Dr. G. Brown Goode, is also called a spinetta à baule. It has a cylindrical hinged cover something like that of a trunk, hence the Italian designation, "baule." The strings are of brass and steel wires, one to each key, and the spines on the jacks are of hard leather. Originally it had four legs, screwed into the body of the instrument.

HARPSICHORD

The harpsichord appeared at about the same time as the spinet and had the same method of tone production, the string being twanged by a quill set in an upright wooden "jack" at the end of the key bar. It was, however, a much more elaborate instrument than the spinet and had two, three, or even four strings to a tone. An early name was "arpicordo," the letter "s" seeming to have been added to the term in England. With three strings it was, of course, necessary to have three jacks and a variety of tone was produced by having two of these of leather and one of stiff quill.

In the sixteenth and seventeenth centuries the harpsichord occupied the place of honor among keyboard instruments which the concert grand piano holds at the present time. It was not so much a solo instrument as the grand piano, but was an important member of the orchestra, having wide and varied resources of tonal effects. Its complex nature, which will be indicated, required a larger case than the spinet and different in shape. To meet this requirement a form was devised which is now the shape of the grand piano.

An outstanding peculiarity of the harpsichord was the use of stops, probably suggested by the organ. These were slides placed above the keyboard and by means of them a wide variety of effects could be produced. For instance, the player could draw out a stop and only the string twanged by the quill would be vibrated, suggesting the sound of a lute. Another stop would cause two of the strings to sound. Some harpsichords had sets of strings of different lengths. A set of long strings produced a 16-foot tone like the long pipes of an organ, another set produced 8-foot tones, another produced 4-foot tones (an octave higher), while some harpsichords had a set of very short strings producing 2-foot tones. The famous Ruckers family, of Antwerp, made harpsichords as well as spinets, continuing the work to the third generation. The greatest harpsichord makers of the eighteenth century in London were Jacob Kirckman and Burkat Shudi, who began business in 1732 in the house which later was occupied by his descendants the Broadwoods, makers of early pianos. Kirckman's harpsichords had a swell, the cover being gradually raised by means of a pedal. Later the organ swell with its shutters was evolved from this appliance. On a harpsichord with two keyboards the upper produced the normal or 8-foot tone, the lower keyboard being used for combinations which were effected by levers pressed by the knees as well as by stops above the keyboard. A particular fine harpsichord (95234) was made by Nicolaus Dequoco in 1693 and obtained in Florence by Doctor Goode in 1892. The body of the instrument is of plain unvarnished wood, and it is enclosed in a painted outer case that rests on a carved gilt stand. It can be removed from the outer case, and that, in turn, may be lifted from the gilt stand. Originally it had three wires to each key, two tuned in unison and the third tuned an octave higher. Originally it had three stops moved by sliding knobs in the face of the name board. These are now missing.

(PIANOFORTE)

The dulcimer, as already indicated, was a percussive instrument, and a larger dulcimer was in a frame with legs at the corners, resembling the frame of a small " square " piano except that it had no keyboard. The strings were struck by hammers held in the player's hands and it had no damping contrivance, so the tone was very harsh. Several attempts were made to combine a keyboard with it during the sixteenth and seventeenth centuries, but the first successful instrument of this sort was invented in 1711 by Bartalomeo Cristofori, a harpsichord maker of Florence. It was called the pianoforte in Italy and the hammerclavier in Germany. Beethoven designated the instrument by both terms. The mechanism for striking the string may be compared to the finger of a violin player, as distinguished from the rigid bar with its upright tangent which characterized the clavichord. At first it was made in wing shape, the oblong frame being introduced in 1779.

"The keyboard instruments then known were nearly or entirely incapable of gradation in the loudness of their tone; hence the new instrument was called a 'piano e forte' because its main peculiarity was that its tone might be made either loud or soft at the player's will." This contrast in tone was produced by the action of two stops, one called "celeste" and producing a soft tone, while the other was called "forte." "Both are divided into two sections, the bass and the treble; each moved independently of the other by four registers on the front side over the keyboard. The chief interest lies in the forte stop which raises the dampers in two sections by two stops." The mechanism does not interest us at present, but we note that it would be possible for a player on this instrument to produce varied effects—for instance, he could give a loud melody in the treble with a subdued accompaniment in the bass. A hammerclavier with a compass of four and a half octaves was made by Johann Christoff Jeckel in Worms in 1783. Some of the early pianofortes varied their tone in the same manner, except that, instead of stops which were pulled out like those of an organ, the variation was accomplished by levers at the player's left hand, or by knee pedals.

These early instruments were "single action." The inventors had achieved the production of loud and soft tones, each half of the keyboard affected independently of the other, but they had not achieved a sustained tone. In an effort to attain this effect there were many unique instruments, in one of which an apparently sustained tone was produced by reiterated blows from small hammers placed above the ordinary hammers and operated by a flywheel controlled by a pedal. All these experiments were laid aside when certain important changes were made in the frame and in the action, or manner of placing the hammer in contact with the string.

The strings in dulcimers and instruments of the spinet group were attached to pegs set in a wooden frame. One of the greatest advances toward the modern piano was the introduction of the iron frame which was patented in 1820 by William Allen, a piano tuner in London, and James Thorne, foreman in a piano factory. The advantage is thus explained by Hopkins: "The greater elasticity of iron as compared with wood does not allow the upper partial tones of a string to die away as soon as they would with the less elastic wood. The consequence is that in instruments where iron or steel preponderates in the framing there is a longer sostenente or singing tone and increasingly so as there is a higher tension or strain on the wire." The belly or sounding board of the piano remained of wood, especially fir wood. Important changes were made in the action as well as in the hammer and in the point at which it struck the string. But the changes in the strings themselves were even more essential to the development of the modern piano. The earliest wire-drawing mill making wire suitable for strings is said to have been at Nuremburg, but about 1820 these strings gave way to Berlin wire. Both these wires were of iron. To Webster, of Birmingham, England, belongs the honor of replacing iron with steel wires in 1834. Careful calculations and practical experiments determined the diameter and tension necessary for strings in the various registers, as well as the "overspinning" or winding of the bass strings. An improvement called "overstringing" was devised about 1830 and consisted in placing the bass division of the strings above the tenor at a divergent angle. This permitted the use of longer strings in the bass section and extended the area of bridge pressure on the sounding board. The method of tuning and the action of the pedals do not concern our present purpose.

Among the famous makers of pianos in the early years of the eighteenth century were Broadwood and Erard, of England, followed by Chickering, of Boston, who patented a new iron frame for square pianos in 1840. The grand piano was patented by Henry Engelhard Steinway, of Steinway & Sons, New York, on December 20, 1859. The modern upright pianoforte was invented by John Isaac Hawkins, an Englishman, who was then living at Philadelphia, Pa., who patented the instrument there and in his native country in 1800. The action was improved by the English maker, Wornum, who patented his model in 1826. Mention should be made of the "cabinet piano" invented in 1807 which did not have an overstrung bass. It was sweet toned, but soon gave way to the modern upright piano.

The present collection includes a model of the old English single action of the piano (95791); of the old German single action (95792); and of the German double action as improved by Streicher in 1892 (95793). Also a model of the Mason & Hamlin patent screw-tuning pins (94650), and a model of the action of an upright piano, patented in 1877 by Albert Steinway (95789).

Among the square pianos exhibited is an instrument made about 1838 (277897). An interesting upright piano was given to the Museum by Mrs. Gouverneur Morris (316176). It it is a Hale piano decorated by Cottier.

The extensive Worch collection of pianos is exhibited on the rotunda balconies of the Natural History Building.

BIBLIOGRAPHY

Among the authorities and catalogues which have been consulted are the following:

ADLER, CYRUS. The shofar, its origin and use. Proc. U. S. Nat. Mus., Washington, D. C., 1893, vol. 16. pp. 287–301.

BALFOUR, HENRY. The natural history of the musical bow. Oxford, 1891.

——— ———. The old British pibcorn or hornpipe and its affinities. Journ. Anthrop. Inst., vol. 20, p. 143. London, 1890.

CASANOWICZ, I. M. The collections of Old World archeology in the U. S. National Museum. Report of Smithsonian Institution for 1922.

DAY, C. R. The music and musical instruments of southern India and the Deccan. Novello, Ewer and Co., London and New York, 1891.

ENGEL, CARL. Researches into the early history of the violin family. Novello, Ewer and Co., London, 1883.

GALPIN, FRANCIS W. Old English instruments of music. London, England, 1910.

——— ———. In Catalogue of the International Loan Exhibition, Crystal Palace, London, 1900.

GALPIN, M. A. The sackbut, its evolution and history. Proc. Musical Asso., 1906–7, (London?), p. 81.

GLEN, J. and R. Historical sketch of the Scotch bagpipe. In Glen's collection for the great highland bagpipe. Edinburgh, n. d.

GROVE. Dictionary of Music and Musicians.

HAWLEY, EDWIN H. Descriptive catalogue of the musical instruments of the world. (in manuscript) Washington.

HIPKINS, A. J. A description and history of the pianoforte and the older keyboard stringed instruments. Novello, Ewer & Co., London and New York, 1896.

HOUGH, WALTER. Synoptic series of objects in the United States National Museum illustrating the history of inventions. Proc. U. S. Nat. Mus., vol. 60, art. 9, 1922.

MASON, OTIS T. Geographical distribution of the musical bow. American Anthropologist, Nov., 1897.

MEAD, CHARLES W. The musical instruments of the Incas. Supplement to American Museum Journal, Amer. Mus. Nat. Hist., New York, vol. 3, No. 4, July, 1903, pp. 12, 13.

MILLER, DAYTON C. Translator's introduction to "The Flute and Flute-playing," by Theobald Boehm. Cleveland, Ohio. 1922.

MORRIS, FRANCES. Catalogue of the Crosby-Brown collection. New ser., vol. 2 (Oceanica and America). New York, 1914.

PIGGOTT, F. T. The music and musical instruments of Japan. London, 1893, pp. 135, 136.

STANLEY, ALBERT A. Catalogue of the Stearns Collection of musical instruments. Ann Arbor, Mich. 1918.

STEINERT, M. Catalogue of the M. Steinert collection of keyed and stringed instruments at the World's Columbian Exposition, 1893.

SWANTON, J. R. Article on Rattles. Handbook of American Indians. Bull. 30. Bureau of American Ethnology.

TAGORE, SOURINDRO MOHUN. Short notices of Hindu musical instruments. Calcutta, India, 1877.

A handbook to the National Museum at the Smithsonian Institution, Washington. Brentano Bros., New York, Chicago, and Washington, 1886.

Catalogues, Crosby-Brown collection of musical instruments, Metropolitan Museum of Art, New York .

A descriptive catalogue of the musical instruments exhibited at the Royal Military Exhibition, London, 1890. London, 1891.

North China Branch, Royal Asiatic Society, 1908.

Catalogue descriptif et analytique du Musee Instrumental du Conservatoire Royal de Musique de Bruxelles. By Victor Charles Mahillon. 1909.

ILLUSTRATIONS

LIST OF ILLUSTRATIONS

PLATE 1

Gongs of jade and metal, and cymbals

114

GONGS OF JADE AND METAL, AND CYMBALS

FOR DESCRIPTION OF PLATE SEE PAGE 114

GONGS OF WOOD AND METAL

FOR DESCRIPTION OF PLATE SEE PAGE 115

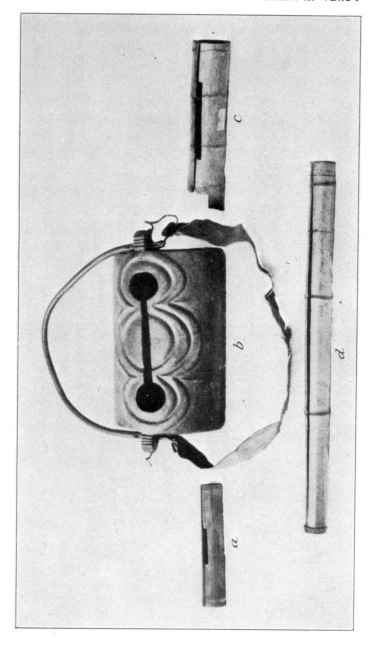

GONGS OF WOOD AND BAMBOO

FOR DESCRIPTION OF PLATE SEE PAGE 116

GONG HARMONIUM, SIAM. WITH FIGURE OF PLAYER

FOR DESCRIPTION OF PLATE SEE PAGE 117

118

BELLS OF METAL AND POTTERY

FOR DESCRIPTION OF PLATE SEE PAGE 118

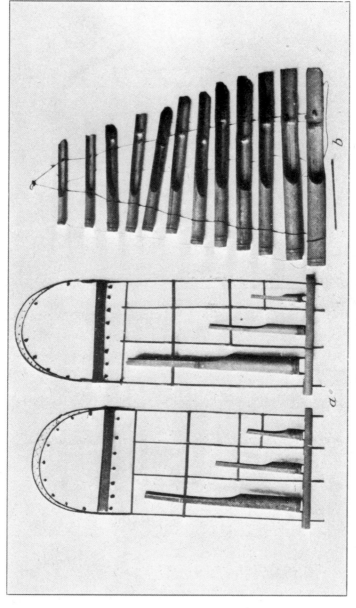

BELLS AND XYLOPHONE OF BAMBOO

FOR DESCRIPTION OF PLATE SEE PAGE 119

PLATE 6

Bells and xylophone of bamboo

PLATE 7

Bells suspended in carved frames

120

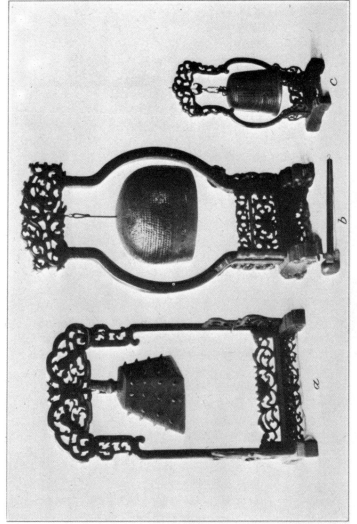

BELLS SUSPENDED IN CARVED FRAMES

FOR DESCRIPTION OF PLATE SEE PAGE 120

RATTLES (HOLLOW AND SONOROUS BODIES)

FOR DESCRIPTION OF PLATE SEE PAGE 121

PLATE 8

Rattles (hollow and sonorous bodies)

121

PLATE 9

Rattles (notched stick and sistrum)

122

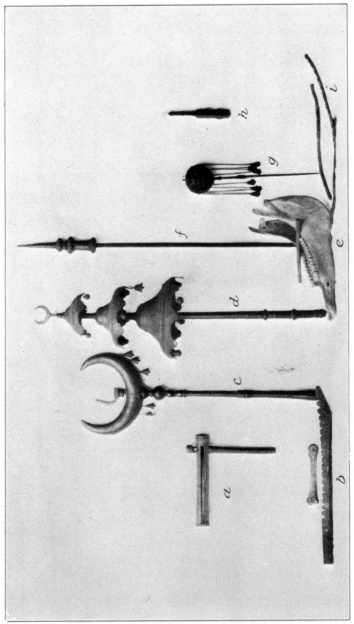

RATTLES (NOTCHED STICK AND SISTRUM)

FOR DESCRIPTION OF PLATE SEE PAGE 122

XYLOPHONES, SIAM AND JAPAN

FOR DESCRIPTION OF PLATE SEE PAGE 123

PLATE 10

Xylophones, Siam and Japan

123

PLATE 11

Marimba, Africa and Guatemala

124

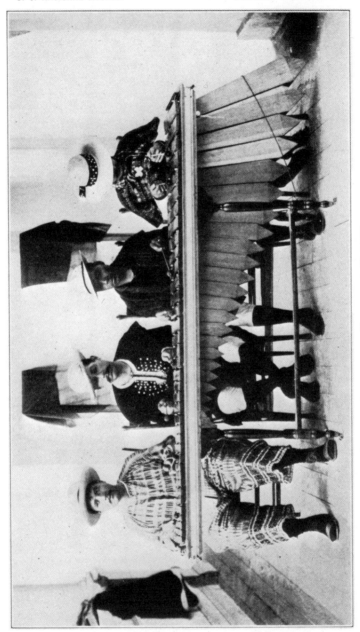

MARIMBA WITH GUATEMALAN PLAYERS

FOR DESCRIPTION OF PLATE SEE PAGE 126

126

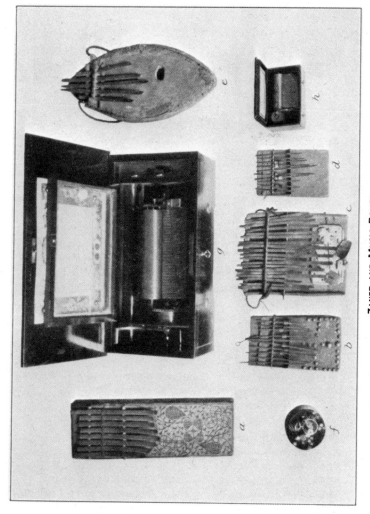

FOR DESCRIPTION OF PLATE SEE PAGE 126

ZANZE AND MUSIC BOXES

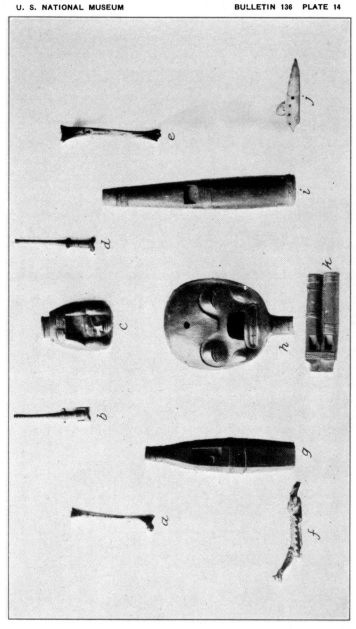

WHISTLES AND FLUTES OF WOOD, BONE, AND POTTERY

FOR DESCRIPTION OF PLATE SEE PAGE 127

PLATE 15

Flutes of cane and wood

128

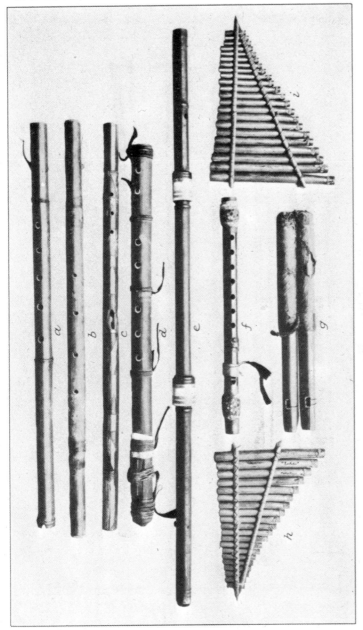

FLUTES OF CANE AND WOOD

FOR DESCRIPTION OF PLATE SEE PAGE 128

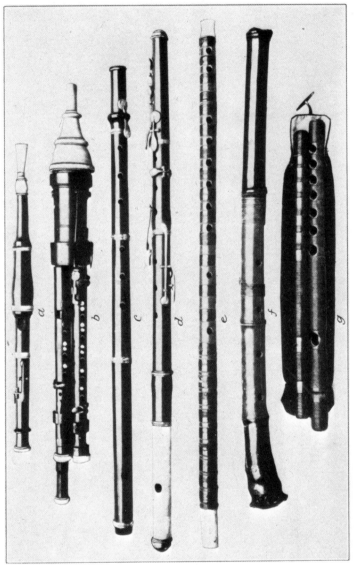

FLAGEOLETS AND FLUTES

FOR DESCRIPTION OF PLATE SEE PAGE 129

130

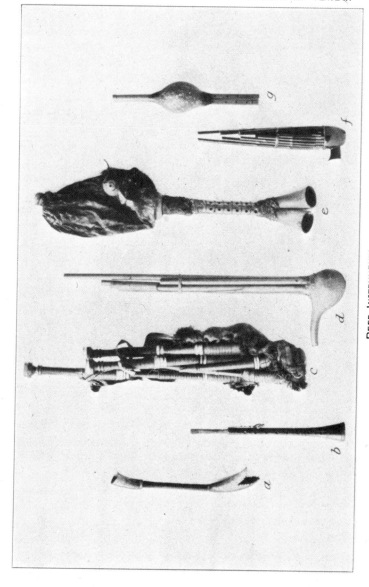

REED INSTRUMENTS

FOR DESCRIPTION OF PLATE SEE PAGE 130

FIGURE OF BAGPIPE PLAYER, ITALIAN PEASANT

FOR DESCRIPTION OF PLATE SEE PAGE 131

PLATE 19 ·

Horns of tusks, animal horns, and shells

132

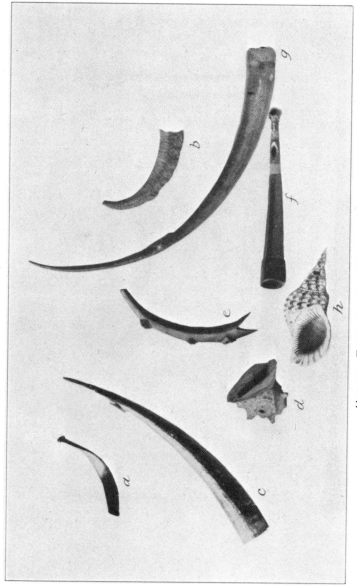

HORNS OF TUSKS, ANIMAL HORNS, AND SHELLS

FOR DESCRIPTION OF PLATE SEE PAGE 132

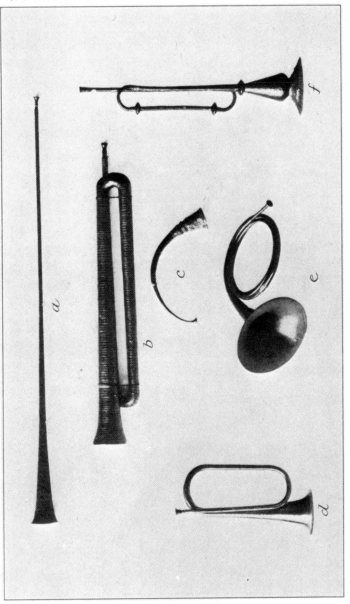

SIMPLE HORNS

FOR DESCRIPTION OF PLATE SEE PAGE 133

PLATE 20

Simple horns

133

134

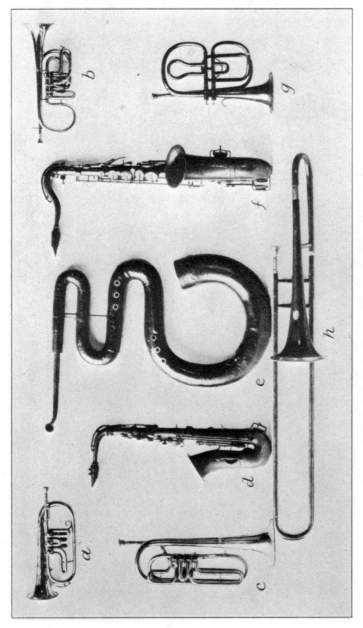

HORNS WITH SLIDE, FINGER HOLES, KEYS, AND VALVES

FOR DESCRIPTION OF PLATE SEE PAGE 134

KETTLEDRUMS CARRIED ON CAMEL, EGYPT

FOR DESCRIPTION OF PLATE SEE PAGE 135

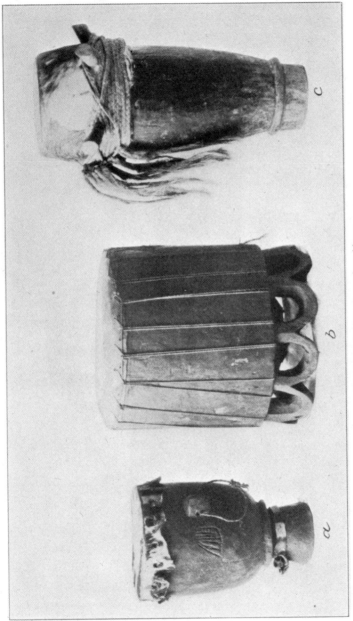

PRIMITIVE DRUMS WITH ONE HEAD

FOR DESCRIPTION OF PLATE SEE PAGE 136

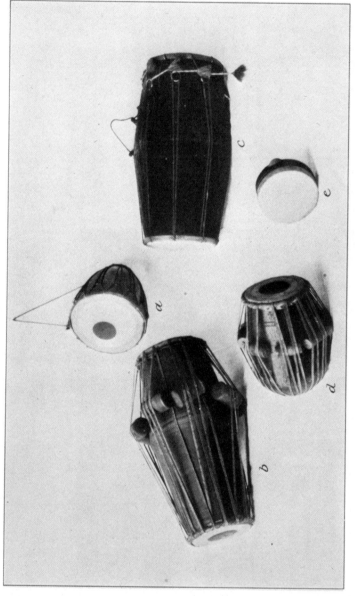

DRUMS AND TAMBOURINE, INDIA

FOR DESCRIPTION OF PLATE SEE PAGE 137

PLATE 24

Drums and tambourine, India

137

 138

VASE-SHAPED DRUMS OF WOOD AND POTTERY

FOR DESCRIPTION OF PLATE SEE PAGE 138

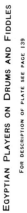

EGYPTIAN PLAYERS ON DRUMS AND FIDDLES

FOR DESCRIPTION OF PLATE SEE PAGE 139

PLATE 27

Primitive drums

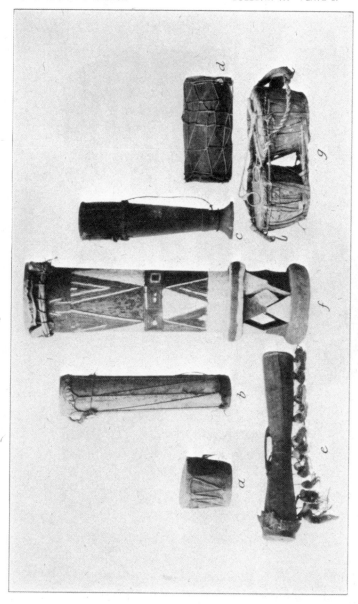

PRIMITIVE DRUMS

FOR DESCRIPTION OF PLATE SEE PAGE 140

For description of plate see page 141

CHINESE, JAPANESE, AND KOREAN DRUMS

PLATE 28

Chinese, Japanese, and Korean drums

141

PLATE 29

Hindu Musicians (p. 67)

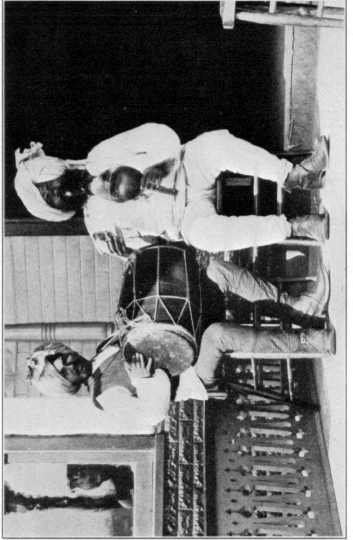

HINDU MUSICIANS

FOR DESCRIPTION OF PLATE SEE PAGE 142

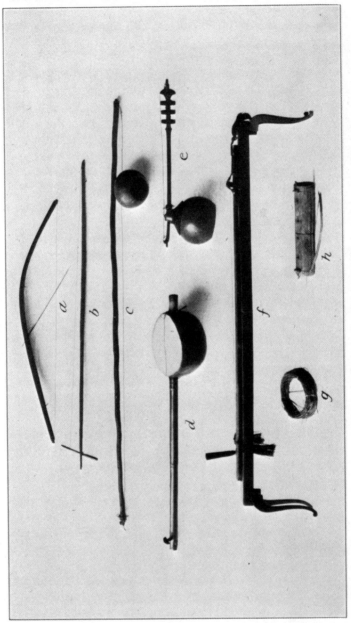

MUSICAL BOW AND ONE-STRINGED INSTRUMENTS

FOR DESCRIPT ON OF PLATE SEE PAGE 143

PLATE 31

Native player on musical bow (p. 31)

NATIVE PLAYER ON MUSICAL BOW

FOR DESCRIPTION OF PLATE SEE PAGE 144

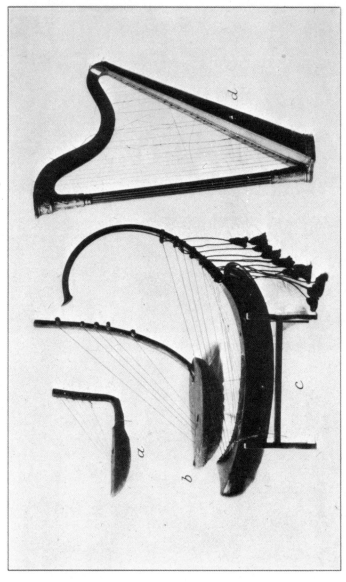

LYRES AND HARPS

FOR DESCRIPTION OF PLATE SEE PAGE 145

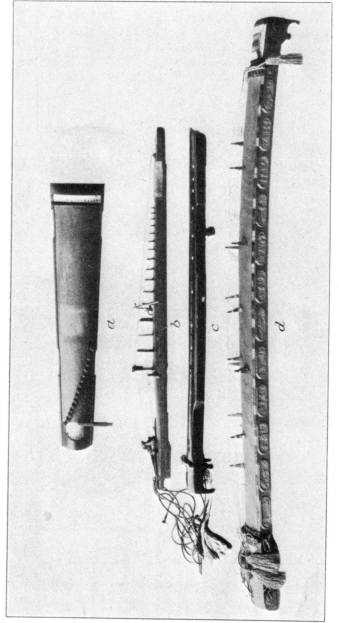

FOR DESCRIPTION OF PLATE SEE PAGE 146

PSALTERY, LUTE, AND KOTO

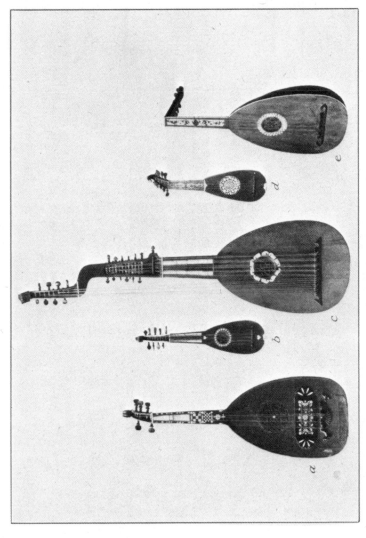

ITALIAN LUTES

FOR DESCRIPTION OF PLATE SEE PAGE 147

PLATE 34

Italian lutes

MANDOLIN AND RELATED INSTRUMENTS

FOR DESCRIPTION OF PLATE SEE PAGE 148

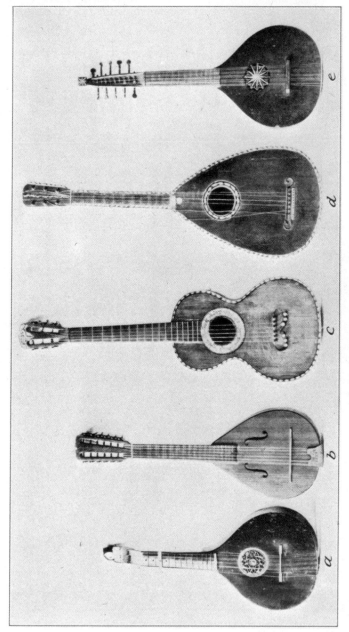

GUITAR AND RELATED INSTRUMENTS

FOR DESCRIPTION OF PLATE SEE PAGE 149

149

PLATE 37

Banjos

150

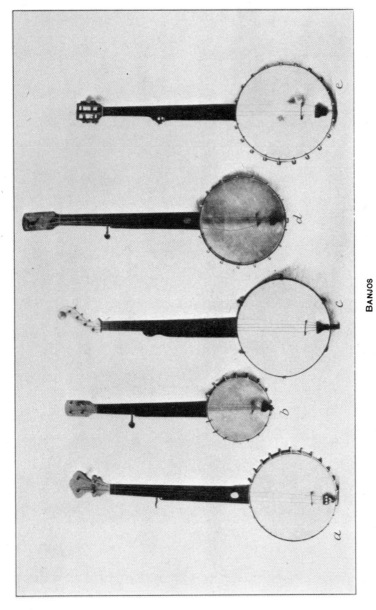

BANJOS

FOR DESCRIPTION OF PLATE SEE PAGE 150

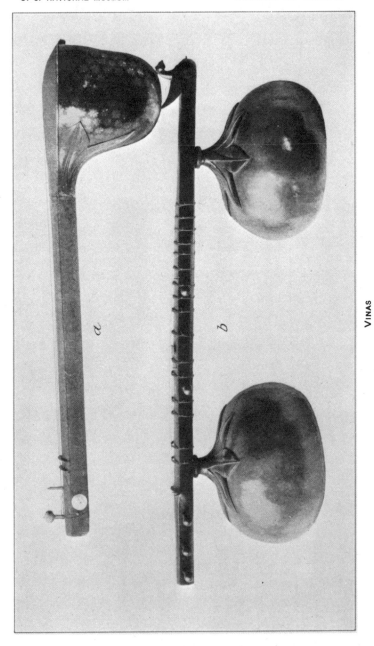

VINAS

For description of plate see page 151

PLATE 39

Vinas

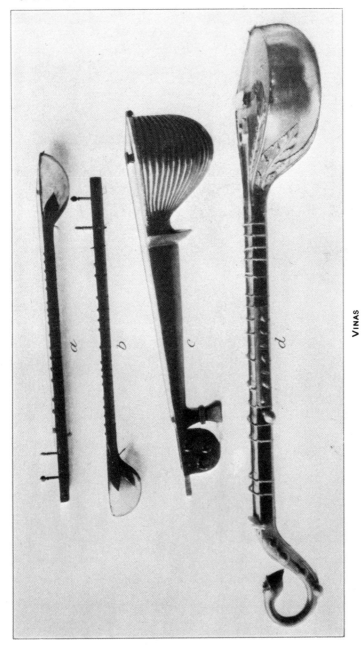

VINAS

FOR DESCRIPTION OF PLATE SEE PAGE 152

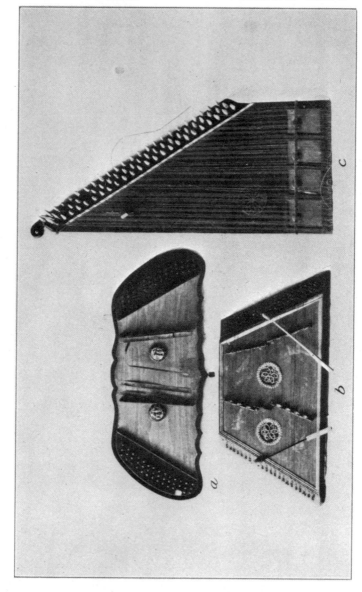

FOR DESCRIPTION OF PLATE SEE PAGE 153

PSALTERY AND DULCIMERS

PLATE 40

Psaltery and dulcimers

153

PLATE 41

Crwth, rebec, viol, and other instruments

154

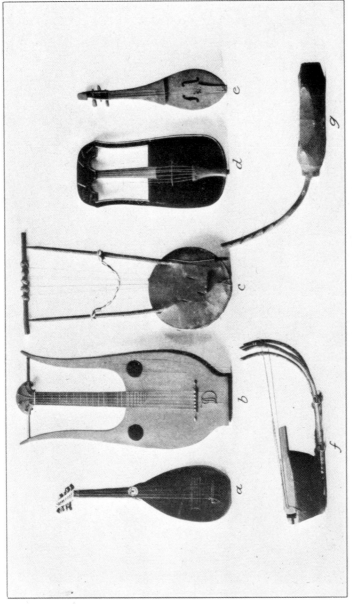

CRWTH, REBEC, VIOL, AND OTHER INSTRUMENTS

FOR DESCRIPTION OF PLATE SEE PAGE 154

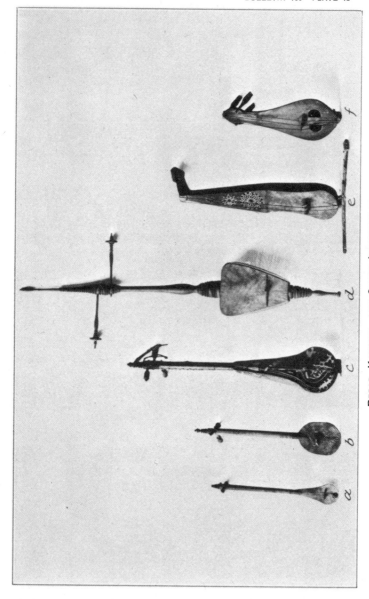

REBAB, KAMANJA, AND OTHER INSTRUMENTS

FOR DESCRIPTION OF PLATE SEE PAGE 155

PLATE 42

Rehab, Kamanja, and other instruments

155

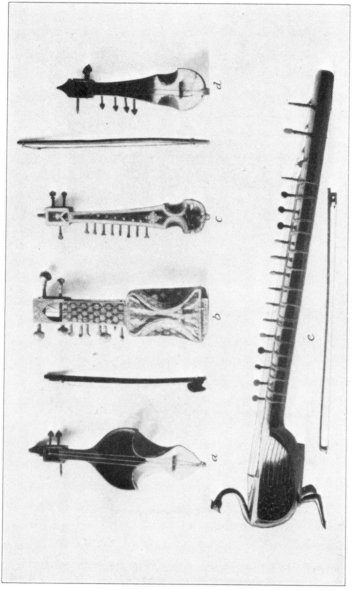

BOWED STRINGED INSTRUMENTS, INDIA

FOR DESCRIPTION OF PLATE SEE PAGE 156

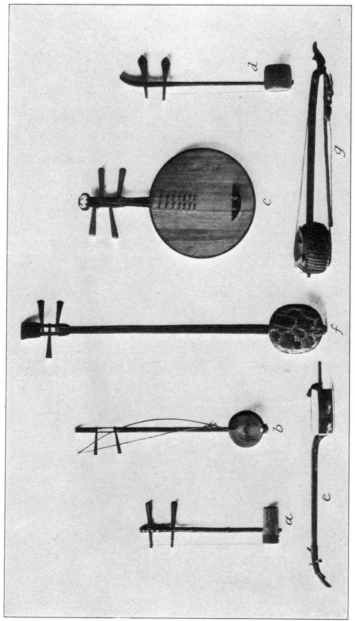

ORIENTAL FIDDLES, BANJO, AND GUITAR

FOR DESCRIPTION OF PLATE SEE PAGE 167

PLATE 44

Oriental fiddles, banjo, and guitar

157

PLATE 45

Apache player on native fiddle (p. 98)

APACHE PLAYER ON NATIVE FIDDLE

FOR DESCRIPTION OF PLATE SEE PAGE 158

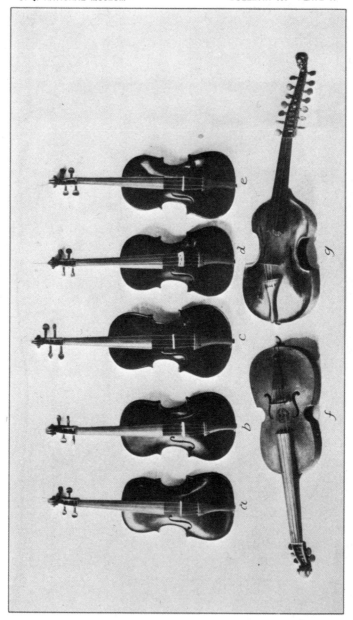

VIOLINS, VIOLA, VIOL D'AMORE, AND VIOL BRACCIA

FOR DESCRIPTION OF PLATE SEE PAGE 159

PLATE 46

Violina, viola, viol d'amore, and viol braccia

159

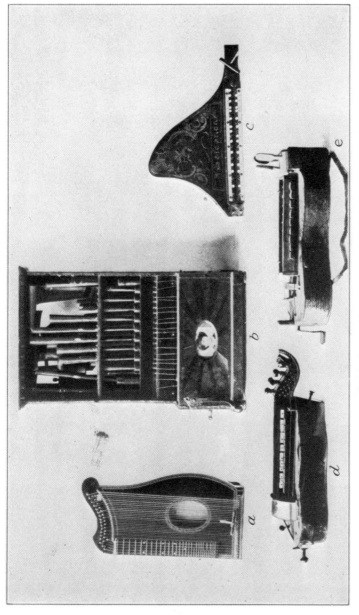

ZITHER, HAND ORGAN, SOLOPHONE, AND HURDY-GURDY

FOR DESCRIPTION OF PLATE SEE PAGE 160

WING-SHAPED SPINET

FOR DESCRIPTION OF PLATE SEE PAGE 181

PLATE 48
Wing-shaped spinet (p. 106)

161

PLATE 49

Virginal (p. 106)

VIRGINAL

FOR DESCRIPTION OF PLATE SEE PAGE 162

INDEX